Moving Up

Moving Up

How to get high-salaried jobs

Eli Djeddah

Ten Speed Press

The resume of "Gary D. Sawyer" is from
How To Make a Habit of Success
by Bernard Haldane (Lee's Summit, Mo.:
Unity Books, 1966, distributed by
Hawthorn Books, Inc., New York, N.Y.)
Reprinted by permission.

Acknowledgment is gratefully
made to ROBERT DE ROOS
for his advice and assistance
in putting this book together.
—E.D.

Beverly Anderson Graphic Design
Printed in the United States of America

Acknowledgments

I am especially grateful to Bernard Haldane Associates, the career counseling firm with whom I have been associated for many years. This organization has provided me with impetus for the development of my ideology, as well as a forum for implementation of the approaches and techniques I recommend in this book. The friendship with Bernard Haldane, Lowell Martin, Richard Germann and other key people are a source of deep inspiration to me.

Contents

1 Setting Your Goals

"Nothing astonishes men so much as common sense."

Ralph Waldo Emerson wrote that more than a hundred years ago, and it is still true. But while it may be astonishing, common sense is your most practical tool for solving life's problems.

With Emerson's remark in mind, let us look at a few other truths:

● Most men and women must earn a living during a large part of their lifetime.

● From time to time these people may be out of work—which is tremendously important to the individuals involved, and their families, but of little or no interest to anyone else.

● Everyone would like to lead a satisfying life, and a great part of any such life is satisfying work.

● Many people are dissatisfied with their work for a simple reason: they are in the wrong job.

So, if you need a job, if you want a better job, if you want to get ahead in your company, this book can help you.

There is no magic in this. It is simply a common-sense approach, and it works. It has worked thousands of times with as many different people. There are no tricks, no gimmicks—just an "astonishing" use of the common sense—the brain power and talents—that you can draw upon if you know how,

You and your goals in life are the subject of this book.
The question of setting personal goals is a very old one, but first a bit of homework, of self-evaluation, is essential.

At the entrance to the Temple at Delphi in ancient Greece, there stood this notice: "Know thyself." In other words, "Please be clear why you are here and why you are asking questions of the Oracle."

A few thousand years later, Shakespeare enlarged this advice: "To thine own self be true, / And it must follow, as the night the day, / Thou canst not then be false to any man."

Constant examination of self should be everyone's concern. We should examine our goals and our purposes continuously throughout our lifetime. Nothing is isolated; everything is part of its frame of reference. It is impossible to have static goals within a changing, moving frame of reference because our purposes are molded by their setting. And there is evidence all around us that "that distant goal selected at the age of twenty can turn out to be a dead end at forty."

"Know thyself."

The statement is easy to quote, but how do you go about it? The way is searching but relatively easy. In advising people who are seeking a position in business, or making a change in their lives, my counseling associates and I ask them to list ten or fifteen of their greatest achievements. To the client who looks blank, we explain: *An achievement is something you are proud of and enjoyed doing.* It does not matter what time of life it comes from: it could be something you took pleasure in during your childhood, your adolescence, or your adulthood; it could be a period of military service, a college experience, an activity in your church, or a hobby you pursued. The content is not important, nor is the impact on others.

Make a list of your achievements. They can be anything as long as they are relevant to you.

"I organized a working committee which streamlined the personnel responsibilities of a sales department; result — increased sales, high morale, and a raise in pay for everyone in the department based on performance."

"I won a national award for technical writing after mastering that difficult art outside the regular responsibilities of my job. This was one of the hardest things I ever did in my life, but it broadened my capabilities with my present company and will serve me wherever I may be employed. More than that, it stretched my ability to the limit, perhaps beyond the limits I had previously set."

"I designed a kitchen arrangement for our home which makes work easier and more pleasant. I also did much of the carpentry work myself, a job I had never tackled before. I was slow, but the job got done."

"After smoking two packs of cigarettes a day for ten years, I gave up smoking. This led me to an examination of all my habits. From this came a more thoughtful arrangement of my life which gives me more time with my family and more time for things I am interested in — tennis, gardening, and especially reading."

"I planned and put on a fashion show to raise money for the college scholarship fund at my daughter's high school. It was such a success that it has become an annual affair, and each year now a deserving graduate is helped to college."

An achievement is something you are proud of and enjoyed doing.

In my counseling firm we take these achievements, these things you are proud of, and analyze them to see what talents they express. We must be careful here because some of the elements involved are inherent in the very nature of the job performed.

For example, if you were the manager of a plant, obviously upper management was involved, planning was involved, and problem solving was involved. What we must determine is *your* talent, as shown by the quality of your performance and the methods of approach used to achieve something that gave you pride and enjoyment.

Draw a line down a sheet of paper. On the left, list all functions that are necessarily a part of your job; on the right, put all things that were your own contribution. Thus on the right we pick up your personal talents, your individual way of performing your job. What were the things which made you a good manager? The ability to inspire others? A talent for creativity, or an endless patience with planning and scheduling? It is by isolating those personal qualities that you learn about yourself.

The process theoretically is quite simple. When you have determined the functions you enjoyed and the personal qualities you exercised in achieving your results, you must then define a goal — a goal which would imply the constant use of the pleasantly effective talents you have discovered. The *level* of your goal will be in accordance with your past experience and progression. It will be determined by your knowledge. It will be affected by your personal considerations. Do you want to become a president of a large corporation? How much time do you want to devote to business? You might conclude as others have done before you that "Man doth not live by bread only" — that the purpose of a job is to support life in its many other manifestations — family, hobbies, the million varieties of things people can be interested in.

Self-analysis can be very revealing. Recently a young man with a master's degree in business administration listed his achievements and, after pondering them and searching their meaning, made a discovery. Whereas he had always thought marketing was his chosen field — indeed, he had been working in marketing with a large corporation — he discovered, in his own words, "that I liked to make money, not only for myself but for other people." His analysis of his list of achievements led him out of marketing and into finance, where he is now happily and profitably engaged. Such a result of the analysis of one's achievements is not at all unusual.

Is it necessary to go to a professional counseling firm to do this? Obviously not. A professional counselor can be useful. There are other approaches, however, which are also helpful.

Professional counseling, based as it is on thousands of cases, often is the quickest way to achieve results when you are making a change in your life, but one purpose of this book is to suggest principles and to demonstrate rules of procedure which will guarantee success in obtaining the position you want without recourse to professional counselors.

When Robert Burns wrote, "O wad some Pow'r the giftie gie us / To see oursels as others see us!" he pointed the way to another tool available to everyone in the process of self examination. A view of yourself as others see you is easily obtainable. Turn to three people who know you well — your wife or husband, your mother, brother, or father, a close friend — and say, "Would you mind writing a letter stating what my greatest talents are, in your opinion, and what you think I would be best suited for?" With three such letters you will be amazed at the insights revealed. The mode of expression will vary, of course, but you generally get back an interesting and accurate picture of yourself as others see you. The answers to your question may not tell you how the qualities your friends or relatives recognize could tie into a job or a career, but these outside views constitute another tool in your self-analysis —the examination of your life.

You can use other supporting evidence, such as interest tests — even psychological tests. Psychological tests, by themselves, are very shaky tools, but when supported by corroborating evidence they become valid.

Now, with a list of achievements before you that indicates what you have enjoyed doing, with statements from those who know you best about your capabilities, and, possibly, with supporting evidence from tests, you have quite a lot of information to aid you in defining your goals. Armed with this material and with a growing knowledge of your direction, it could be profitable and pleasant to talk about yourself to an intelligent friend. You will find you are a very interesting subject to talk about. But you have an obligation here — you must give your friend equal time to talk. This will give you two opportunities to validate yourself — one by your concern with yourself and, second, by your intelligent and valued attentiveness to the concerns of another person.

When I was much younger, I would delight in showing that a mathematical problem could be handled in different ways with equal effectiveness, although not always with equal labor. For instance, a problem which might exercise my brain power to the ultimate to solve arithmetically could often be reduced algebraically and solved rather simply. There are many ways of skinning a cat.

There are many ways of managing, for example. One man might swell out his chest and say, "I'm a beautiful delegator. I don't do anything but sit here all day smoking these expensive cigars." He may be a fine manager, if he has taken care in selecting the people he is going to delegate responsibility to and in monitoring their performance. We all know of brilliant management by delegation.

There is also excellent management by mathematical organization. Many scientists and engineers approach their management problems in a mathematical way. They draw diagrams — functions, flow charts, and all the rest of it — and find mathematical solutions.

Then there is the busybody who does everything alone. There is a limit to this kind of person's performance, but it is much broader than many people would imagine. If he is a human dynamo and very ambitious, a busybody can manage a firm of one or two hundred people, making virtually every decision and doing every major task alone. Such people are not preferred as managers, but if you are that type, recognize it and then measure the limits of your busybodiness — the number of people you can manage and the limits you must impose on your frantic busyness.

What you really want is the answer to the question, "How do I work?" Do you work best by being a CIA agent, snooping around and knowing everything that is going on? Do you work best by praising people and encouraging them to outperform themselves in the service of the common purpose? Do you do your best by brilliant mathematical planning? Do you do it by inventive means, by endless hours of labor, by spurts of genius? What are your characteristics? When you learn them by honest appraisal, you must then try to consider any situation that confronts you and solve it in terms of your strongest powers. Using such an approach, you will discover you can cover an area far greater than might have seemed possible at first.

It is not a cliché to observe that any determination to make a change is an opportunity, an occasion to use your experience to get more of the things you want and have failed to get in the past and to use your knowledge more effectively. All of us, as long as we are alive, can progress in many directions.

To change a job is not at all unusual—the average person's tenure on a job in the United States is 4.8 years. The interval between jobs can be made into a highly productive period in your life if you take the care, the time, and the honesty to evaluate yourself and set reasonable goals for your future.

We all are, of course, subject to various delusions. Let us talk for a moment about a hypothetical case—a man who works for a firm eight years and then is fired. Immediately he suffers from the bitterest disease of all: rejection. "They did not love me," he thinks. "They rejected me." He has to justify himself because of a little rule which is almost a universal law: To ourselves we are all paragons—angels; we are not clowns. As long as we must live with ourselves, we must be comfortable with ourselves in some manner.

Now, our man has been rejected and his first reaction—whether he just whispers it or shouts it to his wife—is to say, "Those damn fools don't know what they're doing. They did this wrong and that wrong and a lot of other things wrong. They're no good."

Then, a moment later, he thinks, "Well, I can't really say that. If they are no good, I must be more stupid than they, because I worked for them eight years. So they are really good. They are a fine company, because I can't be wrong and I worked for them eight years."

Now he has a new problem. How does he handle it? "Was I really a bad engineer?" he asks himself. "No, of course I'm not a bad engineer. The real truth of the matter is that I'm not really interested in engineering. I'm in the wrong field. That's what's the matter. I'll look up some ads in the *Wall Street Journal* and I'll call on a couple of counseling firms and let them redefine me.

"I never was interested in engineering. It was only because my Uncle Jim, damn him, persuaded me to go to M.I.T. that I ever became an engineer. It was a bad decision made when I was too young to know any better. I should have been a lawyer. No, I really shouldn't have been a lawyer because Uncle Harry's a lawyer and he's no good, either. I should have been . . . well, maybe a doctor, but it's a little late for that now. But I still have time to be a chiropractor. That only takes two years. I understand chiropractors make good money. I'll go to a counselor. . . ."

This man is kidding himself, but all of us kid ourselves:

We see this situation frequently in our counseling work. A client comes in and says, "I have been an engineer for eight years, but I'm in the wrong field." So we tell him, "Let us analyze the problem and find out what your field should be. Will you kindly go home and write out your fifteen greatest achievements?"

The man makes out his list and it reads something like this: "Built an impossible bridge over an improbable river, saved $400,000 in steel cost. Was first to use nylon cords to suspend a bridge. Received a commendation from the Society of Bridge Builders. Was awarded Patent No. 265399 for a new optical device to scan the heavens. . . ."

He reads these achievements and says, "What do you mean I'm not a good engineer? Look at this list. Who's got the nerve to say I'm not an engineer? The trouble was that I didn't have enough engineering responsibility. I'm absolutely brilliant. Those people just didn't recognize it. . . ." And he no longer believes he should make a change because he is in the wrong field. Habit is a powerful master. It is unlikely that anyone can do something for many years and still be miscast. There may be some temporary difficulty — generally on the human level, rather than the job level — but the field is correct.

Once you have become better acquainted with yourself and have more knowledge of your talents, achievements, and goals, you can begin to think seriously of ways and means to get the job you want. I will take you through a market campaign — a way of selling your abilities and potentials at the highest possible level. This campaign will be tied together by a series of letters and a carefully constructed résumé. It will take you to newspaper advertisements, employment agencies, job recruiters, and the top executives of your community and, possibly, of your own company. It will get you the job you want.

I repeat: You must get off to a good start. You cannot organize an effective campaign unless you master the elements in this chapter. You must recognize and analyze your achievements, your manner of working, and the goals you pursue. From this analysis, your personal talents and needs will emerge. Supplement your own analysis with the outside views of relatives and friends — the people who know you best. Talk about yourself with a respected friend. Recognize the areas in which you can use your strongest abilities. "Know thyself." Once you know your talents, the way you work best, the goals you seek, you can take the next step — writing an effective résumé that will represent you in shining colors.

2 Making Your Résumé Work for You

When you have listed your achievements and gained from them a better understanding of where your talents lie and the areas in which you enjoy working, you are faced with the necessity of proving your conclusions in an objective way—in the job market. One excellent entrée here is through a résumé. Almost everyone recognizes the résumé as a sales tool, a device to sell what you have to other people. There is more to it than that: Your résumé's first sale must be to yourself. Properly constructed, it should be a photograph of you at your most focused point. It should be the written proof of the validity of your conclusions about yourself.

If you put your conclusions and your goals down on paper and everything adds up in a manner that is practical, convincing, logical, and reasonable, there is obviously a high probability that the goals you have set are proper. If the goals do not relate to the proofs behind them, surely the résumé cannot be correct. Suppose you construct an inaccurate résumé, but you're so enamored of your writing that you cannot see the errors. It would take only a visit or two for some executive to point out the discrepancies. Better that a friend point them out first. A bad résumé does a bad job.

A résumé should do a number of things. First, it should set forth as clearly as possible the objective you have in mind *in terms of other people's interests*. No end is worthwhile that is self-oriented. The only valid and positive goals are those that match the interests and needs of others. Let us sample a badly constructed résumé, that of a fine young man with considerable talent. He was a lieutenant in the Army, about to leave the service, and he wrote on his résumé that his objective was "A position of responsibility in management which will use my education and my organizational abilities in the management of complex projects."

This is a statement which may have delighted the young lieutenant, but it will delight no one else. It is nonsense. He is coming out into the world and he is fixing conditions while soliciting a job. He is saying, "You have to recognize my education, you have to recognize my organizational abilities,you have to put me in charge of the management of some complex project, and then, when you have done all these things for me, at your risk and peril, I'll give it a try."

You have to state in your résumé what you are going to provide for the world. Only when you identify with other people's interest will there be any interest whatsoever in you.

So the first thing about a résumé is that it is an hypothesis: *This is what I propose to be.* Then it should go into your background to pick up the supporting elements. If you propose to be an engineer, you should show immediately that you have been prepared in engineering by some college or university and list your education. If you have any related work experience, add it. If you are a copywriter, artist, illustrator, advertising manager, designer, photographer, reporter, or in any field where your expertise or art leads to the production of tangible or visible end products of displayable or easily transportable size, a portfolio or display case that would interlock with your résumé should be carefully prepared. This provides not merely strong but indispensable support to the statements your résumé contains.

A résumé should state a purpose and connect it to the *related* parts of your background only. All other material is irrelevant. You must not lie, you must not distort, but you are entitled to show yourself at your very best. The résumé must be brief. It must provoke questions. You do not tell a prospective employer everything about yourself. If he is interested, he will question you. On the first page, there should be a statement of your goal supported by relevant facts about your education and job experience, personal data (although you are no longer required to provide this information, you may wish to include age, marital status, health, hobbies, and a list of relevant affiliations with professional or trade societies). On a second page: "Related achievements."

Your achievements must be collected on a *separate* page to permit them the full effect of their special function in your résumé. Achievements trigger interest. They trigger not only an intellectual response in the reader but also an emotional response. After all, if I manufacture sandbags and you have listed as an achievement that you sold sandbags at a price 14 percent higher than the market, I will become emotionally excited no matter how clinical I want to be in my approach to you as a candidate for employment. The prospect of being able to be greedy, of being able to sell my sandbags at a higher price if I employed you, would be exciting to me.

Your achievements should be grouped in the form of an inverted triangle. You start at the top with the broadest achievement and end with the narrowest. Say you have identified your area of functional abilities as management, technical knowledge, and creativity. Then you would take these capabilities in that order: your management ability first, technical ability second, creativity third, ability to handle people fourth, and so on down the scale. When appropriate the achievement page can be supplemented with a paragraph qualified in the margin by the words "Quotes by Others" or "Comments by Others" as illustrated in a number of the sample résumés. You have probably now discovered that a résumé is a blend of facts, opinions and promises. The inexperienced will have more promises and opinions than facts. Experienced people will have more facts than promises and opinions.

The other effect of such a listing is this: it acts as a kind of sieve. If you want a position as an engineer, you have covered your background and most of the areas that would interest someone interested in employing engineers. When such a man reads your achievements, he will stop at any one that relates to problems he may be faced with. Then his interest will be aroused, perhaps emotionally, and he will begin to ask you questions.

There are many reasons to present a résumé in this style. One reason is that, if you use only materials relating to your purpose, you avoid the danger of having to speak outside the area of your interests. You have limited the terrain. You have defined the ground on which the discussion will take place. Second, the use of a descending order of functions and abilities enables a prospective employer to recognize and evaluate your talents without your prompting. Third, it gives you absolute self-confidence, because you have constructed a résumé which is true, which shows you in your best light, and which represents you as a focused individual. Anyone who is self-confident does not receive "validation" questions. This kind of person gets only "relevancy" questions. Relevancy questions lead to jobs. Validation questioning is an examination which very few people succeed in passing.

Here are excerpts from a résumé of an applicant whose purpose was to become employed as business development manager—with some interpolated remarks:

Résumé: *Qualified to work in an area where proven abilities in creative sales management, product development, market analysis, recruiting and training of personnel, sound business judgment, success in motivating and negotiating at all levels would contribute to increased profits and an enhanced corporate image.*

Executive: Hm, that's a fairly big job.

Résumé: *Originated and defined the position. Was responsible for sales management, product distribution, manuscript development, negotiations with members of college and university faculties in eleven western states; supervised the staff of thirty* *sales, clerical, and warehouse personnel. Sales volume increased 35 percent in eighteen months.*

Executive: Hey!

Résumé: *Further experience as director, business and sale promotion at the PDQ Theater Center, Dallas, Texas, and the LMN Music Theaters, etc.*
Education: BA in communication.
Age: 46.
. . .

Devised and implemented [followed by a series of eight fantastic money-producing stories. . . .]

Which really add up to "once upon a time there was this good magic creature from another world who did a lot of brave things and overcame any number of difficulties and lived happily ever after." The people reading all this are narcotized into this fairy-tale world and they think, "Golly this couldn't possibly be true." But they look up and see in front of them a smiling, radiant, self-confident person and they think, "Well, could it be true? Let's question this applicant a little bit."

Executive: I don't see how you could possibly have made two hundred and ten thousand dollars in eight months when the company had in the prior two years lost money. Tell me how you did that.

Our friend was waiting for this opportunity, of course. He had all the answers.

To show you the effect that properly worded achievements can have, there is a little experiment which works generally on about 80 percent of my lecture audiences. I would like to try it with you.

Imagine that you are walking somewhere in the countryside along a shady country lane. You see a cottage; near the entrance, there is a rosebush with one beautiful red rose. You are startled by the play of sunlight on the color of the flower, and you hesitate; then you slowly bend down to smell the flower to see if it is real. Bend toward the rose and smell its perfume.

This experiment is usually conducted before a group of people. I ask them to close their eyes while I recite the paragraph above and to open their eyes when they smell the rose. Perhaps you can close your eyes and relive the little story and discover how soon you will smell the flower.

About eight out of ten people tested actually smell the rose. One day a man I tried this on said, "I didn't smell it."

I said, "Well, maybe you're not like me; you wouldn't bend down to smell a rose. So let me walk you into the kitchen of that cottage. On the kitchen table, there is a knife and an onion. The onion has been sliced down the center and its juicy, concentric rings are exposed to the light. Will you bend your head forward to it? Your nose is in the onion. Will you smell it and open your eyes when you get the smell?"

About sixty seconds later he triumphantly opened his eyes and cried, "Hah! I caught you. I have no sense of smell."

I said, "Would you mind wiping the tears off your cheek? Your eyes are watering."

These results show that the power of suggestion is very great. Your résumé is also affected by the power of suggestion which, if you are stating fact, is then confirmed by any other conversation you may have.

Following are samples of résumés
which meet all requirements:

I. [*the first page*]   [Name]
                              [Address]
                              [Tel. No.]

FINANCIAL EXECUTIVE

Qualified by:

Over fifteen years of experience as chief financial officer with additional administrative responsibilities. Assignments have required close familiarity with technical, manufacturing, marketing, and public relations functions, and close support to general management.

Experience:

TREASURER-CONTROLLER, XYZ Corporation. Producer of telephone systems and components. Complete responsibility for reorganizing all areas of financial planning, management, and controls and supporting interlocks with manufacturing and marketing.   (1972-present)

CONTROLLER-DIRECTOR OF ADMINISTRATION, ABC Company. Provides security information services to financial community. Responsible for organizing effective records, procedures, and controls to reverse negative cash flow and place company on profitable basis. Made Director of Administration to improve operational effectiveness.   (1970-1972)

TREASURER, JKL Company. Responsible for initiating the financial methods, procedures, and controls for new technical manufacturing company. Assumed responsibility for contracts, administration, purchasing, industrial relations, and industrial engineering.   (1961-1969)

CORPORATE MANAGER OF GENERAL ACCOUNTING, X Corporation. Promoted to this position in less than six months from Chief of Financial Systems and Procedures. Reorganized accounting and financial management to generate the money and controls suited to a sudden corporate expansion.

(1958-1961)

Education:

MBA, areas of interest—finance and manufacturing, Stanford University. AB, Economics, Stanford University.

Personal:

Age 49—married—excellent health.

[*the second page*]

EFFECTIVENESS

Management:

As GENERAL ACCOUNTING MANAGER for X Corporation, which was suffering from the complications of a meteoric growth from $20 million to over $200 million in a three-year period, developed and implemented the complex interlocking procedures and controls to make payables and receivables current, improve corporate image, and create the first cash surplus in corporate history.

Corporate long-range planning highlighted the need for diversification away from major military system contracts. Identified, researched, proposed, with a complete study, the activation of a dormant group of state-of-the-art electronic components products into an autonomous division. Was entrusted with broadest controllership and administrative authority to make the dominant factor in the semiconductor field within one year.

Systems/Methods/Controls:

Together with four associates, spearheaded the studies, prospectus, and organizational requirements and secured $3.1 million initial financing to establish the electronic component company. As key administrative officer, provided the tools and management to generate $20 million per annum, including a long-term $50 million contract.

When XYZ Corporation was operating under the double pressure of $3 million ninety-day loans and an operating loss, reorganized and implemented procedures and controls to stem cash drain, enhance credit image, and provide the structured support for a profitable operation.

Was called upon by ABC Company to assume the financial and related administrative services to provide the basis for growth in capacity and additional working capital. Implemented this assignment and provided the cash flow required to double volume, pay increased dividends, accelerate tax payments, provide $800,000 cash surplus, and support a 100 percent increase of business in three years.

Resourcefulness:
Through the development and implementation of controls and accurate cost-accounting methods, provided major contribution to increase earnings from 8 to 14 percent.

Through improved information and forecasts, increased inventory turnover to more than three times per annum.

II. [*the first page*]

[Name]
[Address]
[Tel. No.]

PERSONNEL TRAINING AND DEVELOPMENT

Qualified by:
Over ten years of growing responsibility in teaching, training, organizing, and motivating as sergeant of Marines, a teacher of English, an athletic trainer, and a leader in scouting.

Education:

Teaching Credential, the University of California.

Selected from three thousand for a $10,000 teaching scholarship, Graduate Internship Program (A–average).

BA, San Francisco State College (Dean's List).

Major: English. Minor: Physical Education.

Eagle Scout, BSA; Senior Patrol Leader; at 13, second youngest in State of California.

Water Safety Instructor, American Red Cross.

Experience:

Teacher of English — Sports Coach. Taught five classes of English to different grade levels and ability groupings; advised junior, senior classes; coached AAU swimming team, school tennis team. Member, curriculum council, accreditation committee; treasurer, faculty club.   (1973-present)

Concurrently with education, acted as salesman in retail store; lifeguard/swimming instructor.   (1967-1973)

Sergeant, United States Marine Corps. Class II Reserve.
                                                    (1971-present)

Personal:

Age 26, married, 6'0", 155 lbs., excellent health.

Hobbies:

Sailing, swimming, tennis, music, creative writing.

Affiliations:

Dolphin Swimming and Boating Club.
Marines' Memorial Association.
California Coaches' Association.
Hayward Area Concert Association.

EFFECTIVENESS

Management:
Responsible for organization and production of infantry battalion Operation Plan for a four-day field exercise, including maneuvering more than 1,000 troops and coordinating fire of supporting arms (air and artillery).

As faculty adviser to the senior class, worked effectively as mediator between class leaders and school administrators; helped develop a class theme and related ideas involving organization of large numbers of students who had never before participated in class activities.

Teaching/Training:
Brought school tennis team from last place in league standings to a tie for fourth place in one year through long hours of skills and strategy coaching and building team spirit.

Possess current Red Cross Water Safety instructor certification; have taught a variety of aquatic skills from beginning swimming to sailing and small craft safety.

Communications:
Received commendations from principal's office, department head, and parents for consistently generating enthusiasm in classroom activities through use of a wide variety of teaching methods and training aids.

Published article on coaching debating in a professional journal during first year of teaching.

Public Relations:
As junior and senior class adviser, suggested and helped develop a number of fund-raising projects to defray a percentage of the cost of senior activities, making participation possible for all.

[Name]
[Address]
[Tel. No.]

A RESPONSIBLE POSITION IN MANAGEMENT

Qualified by:

Over fifteen years proven experience in defining and scheduling total program requirements in a multiplicity of areas; adept at effective and efficient follow-through to ensure accomplishment.

Experience:

CONSULTANT, QRS Data Services, Inc. Primary responsibilities in the sale and development of computer systems, particularly in the areas of design, documentation, implementation, project costing/budget preparation, and proposal writing. Systems included were in Personal Trust Accounting (IBM 360/30 — DOS disc), Investment Portfolio Management, Subscription Fulfillment, Accounts Payable, Dun & Bradstreet on-line interface (utilizing Western Union ASR through IBM 047), Certificate Number/Share Holding Conversion.   (1975-present)

SYSTEMS CONSULTANT, Y & Y Associates. Responsibilities in system project sales including functioning as Project Manager in preliminary analysis, organization, and implementation. This involved working with IBM 360 COBOL (conversion of COBOL programming from IBM 7040 to 360/50) and the design and implementation of MIS system which combined COBOL F and FORTRAN IV on such systems as Source and Application of Funds, Open-Order Accounts Receivable, and Sales Reporting and Market Analysis.   (1974-1975)

EDP MANAGER, John Jones Media. Organized, established, and directed the Computer Department involving twelve technicians utilizing the large-scale H-200 (32K CP, 7 tapes, HSP, etc.), the small-scale H-200, and the special purpose A.B. Dick Videograph. Planned and initiated a Subscription Fulfillment system handling three million subscribers for fourteen magazines (two with over one million subscribers each).   (1970-1974)

SYSTEMS REPRESENTATIVE, Smith, Inc. Responsible for the preparation of written proposals based on systems analysis and design, feasibility studies, conversion problem analysis, and computer configuration. Further responsible for the presentation of these to management. (1968-1970)

Additional experience includes STAFF CONSULTANT for X Corp., MANAGER OF STATISTICAL INFORMATION at the Y Fund, Inc., PROGRAMMER for the Z Corporation and frequent consulting assignments for special projects.

Education:
BA (Psychology/Philosophy) — University of Missouri.
Postgraduate concentration (Industrial Psychology and Economics) — New York University, Syracuse University.
Member — Psychology Department, Syracuse University.

[*the second page*]

EFFECTIVENESS

Management:
Enabled John Jones Media to realize an annual saving of $100,000 by organizing, establishing, and directing a Computer Department handling over three million subscribers. This was accomplished without backup since the Computer Service Bureau refused to provide this function. Time required from initiation to full operational level — 17 months.

Within period of ninety hours completed a proposal (including an analysis of conversion problems, manual systems flow and forms layout, computer systems flow and forms layout, file designs and program specifications, manpower and space requirements, and an implementation schedule) converting certificate numbers and share holding for 3.6 million accounts (representing 86.4 million certificates) from manual ledger cards to a computer-formatted and balanced file. This was accomplished after only six hours of discussion and ledger record examination.

Methods:

Following a preliminary analysis, thoroughly researched the field of Personal Trust Accounting and designed a new system totally comprehensive in scope and function. This was accomplished within a period of five months and included a 300-page system and program documentation report.

Designed a Management Information System (Real-Time) used in the processing of funds (source and application) with the capacity to change program functions without reprogramming. This system provided totally confidential information to each division of a major oil company on an independent basis.

Resourcefulness:

Effected a net direct cost savings of $42,000 per year through systems design resulting from research in the performance of subscription fulfillment.

Produced in-depth analyses and evaluations through feasibility studies in unresearched areas. Examples: (a) Registration of six million pedigreed animals, (b) Real-Time scheduling of auto maintenance and related files, (c) Real-Time credit card accounting, (d) Source and Application of Funds.

Communications:

Commended by the Blank Club at the conclusion of a whole-day presentation for the clear manner used in handling technical data and the proposed utilization of this material. This was one of many proposals of varied types presented in conferences and whole-day sessions at which I was the only woman attending.

Personal:

Age 41, single, health excellent.

"All well and good," you say, "for men and women represented by these résumés — people with a background of work experience. But I am twenty-four years old, just coming out of the

Navy, with no real job experience. What do I do?" The answer is illustrated by the effective résumé below, its style of presentation adapted to the circumstances:

Age: 24	GARY D. SAWYER
Married	Tel.: CIrcle 6-8212
Veteran	59 Grace Court
BA, Yale	Drexel Hill

Objective:
SELLING OR SALES PROMOTIONAL WORK—Where use can be made of contact making and persuasive abilities; ingenuity in originating and developing ideas; manual skill and understanding of mechanisms—talents that would be useful in demonstrating, troubleshooting, or technical sales.

SOME INDICATIONS OF POTENTIAL VALUE

Salesmanship Qualities:
Have always been able to meet people easily and have exhibited persuasive abilities on worthwhile subjects. For example: As a camp counselor instituted changes in activities of a group of 50 boys that provided more continuous events and more broadening experiences. Doing this involved persuading camp owner and 12 other counselors that the results justified the extra work involved. As a community chest solicitor obtained my quota first out of 200 solicitors; then exceeded quota by 85%. . . . Worked up and performed a college radio program that drew favorable response. . . . Originated routines and trained a three-man team of song leaders that appeared before crowds of 70,000.

Leadership:
Through a series of contests and awards, instructing and inspecting, produced a record for camp cleanliness that owner said was the best in 25 years. . . . Directed 50 boys and 15 counselors in organizing and producing a carnival that was voted best in the history of this event.

Management:
>Managed camp laundry; had charge of soft drink sales in Navy barracks; coached college soccer team.

Ideas:
>Invented a device used by skiers that has been copied and used by professionals; devised a humidifying system for a large residence.
>
>Composed words and music for more than fifteen popular and classical songs; planned weekly radio programs; wrote and staged puppet shows.

Writing:
>Wrote story for publication throughout all-Navy WTS program schools; was in top 5% in short-story class, in top quarter of class in theme writing.

Manual Skills:
>Rank in 98th percentile on manual dexterity. Designed and built "home workshop projects"; repaired radios and mechanical equipment for puppet shows. Worked on building repairs and construction crew; laid bricks, wooden floors, linoleum, glazed windows.

Employment:
>Held summer jobs as camp counselor; laborer on factory maintenance crew; construction and surveying.

By directing prospective employers to his potentialities in the areas of salesmanship, leadership, management, ideas, writing, and manual skills this young man presented himself in such a favorable light—within the truth—that he received seventeen replies from twenty résumés sent out and three job offers, one of which he accepted.

In the résumés that have been presented, one element is paramount; each person was in focus; each person directed the résumé toward a desirable position in a fairly well-defined area and felt that he or she could be of value to the companies approached. Focus is absolutely necessary in your job search. It not only must be visible in your résumé but be a functioning part of your attitude at every step of the way. It is a subject I will illustrate more fully in the next chapter, along with other personal and practical suggestions to you in your campaign.

The above résumés are not exhaustive of problems and concerns facing individuals but do indicate how such problems can be intelligently handled.

Ten additional sample résumés are provided in the Appendix starting on page 157. They illustrate other ways of presenting one's background, and they suggest how to deal with special problems such as career change, inexperience and/or unrelated experience, inadequate formal education, too many jobs, too few jobs, or unpaid activities.

3 Preparing Yourself and Your Attitudes

There are several aspects to developing the kind of personal attitude about yourself and your goals that equips you to perform at your very best level as you embark on your job campaign. Your preparation for this star performance can be compared with the training of an athlete for an important sporting event. He knows he must not only get his body in shape but sharpen himself spiritually and mentally as well. His attitude must be just right. His mind must be alert and flexible. When all three parts of his being — physical, spiritual, and mental — are at their radiant best, he will be fully prepared to accomplish his purpose, whether it is winning the decathlon or getting a new job.

Note the word "purpose." Talent, experience, academic background, and brains are not by themselves guarantees of any kind of success in your career — more than in intermittent flashes. Without a goal, those qualities mean very little. As we have seen, goals are developed by a constant process of examination and re-examination. Something which seems right at a certain time may need to be reinterpreted and modified in a few years. You probably will not have to seek a completely different goal but only change its shape somewhat. A purpose you state today relates to the world of today. When the world changes, your purpose has to change with its new frame of reference.

Your first step, then, is to examine and define your purpose in today's terms. Next, you add the muscle of discipline to condition and focus all your forces in the direction of that goal. And this means *all* your forces — your physical self, your mental self, your spiritual or emotional self. You condition all three.

For your physical well-being, exercise is important. If you can't play golf or tennis daily, perhaps you can walk to wherever you're going; if you can't walk every day, you can spend a few minutes doing exercises from one of the numerous physical fitness systems available in books or from your doctor. And if you're overweight, go on a diet, again with your doctor's blessing.

There are a number of ways to exercise your mind; a bridge game, a chess game, a crossword puzzle, even a friendly argument will keep the brain agile. Another way is to undertake a plan of continuous inquiry into some subject that interests you. I do not mean that you should rush to college extension courses to get a degree. That is sometimes just an evasion, an indication that you don't know what to do with yourself. And actually you may find that you need not stress the mental side of your conditioning at all; your present job itself, unless it is so repetitious that it has reduced much of your mental activity to a subconscious level, may well be keeping you mentally vigorous.

Emotional or spiritual fitness is a large and highly individual subject, and I won't attempt to cover it here. But one way to keep emotionally fit is to be helpful to others. When we are effective social animals, we generally feel emotionally at ease. Another way to achieve that ease is to translate your thoughts into action; if your thoughts are purposeful, your actions will express that purpose and you will have the satisfaction of continuing progress toward the goals you have set. Inactivity destroys confidence.

Activity maintains it: activity with a purpose, that is.

The first and foremost necessity in the implementation of goals is planning. *A purpose without a plan is purely a wish.* So if you have not organized your planning, I suggest you do.

As a helpful organizing device, I myself use a thing called the Caddylak Pocket Memo System. This little folder enables me to carry money and credit cards; it has a space for a yearly calendar and a little booklet for telephone numbers. And it provides a set of monthly diaries with a page for every day.

On a normal day, I divide the right-hand page into hours and mark down the ineluctable events, those things which have been decided previously—the appointments I have at various hours. On the left, I mark down those things I hope to accomplish during that day. If any of these items are left over, I move them to the next day; they remain in the book until accomplished. Now, if there are future events to watch for—say I write a letter to Mr. Blank today and want a response from him by the 15th of next month—I pick up next month's diary and mark on the 15th, "Check for Blank's report." I have a little tick list going; I have a diary in retrospect; I have a list of things to be accomplished day by day.

In daily affairs, yours and mine and everybody's, the human being is essentially a dreamer, awake or asleep. We are born like philosophers and disorganized dreamers. We sometimes need an assist of some sort to turn our thoughts into actions. If we were to raise our efficiency from 1 to 10 percent, we would be demigods. So it is with this sneaky purpose in mind that I plant upon my person a planning device.

When I write down the things I want to accomplish on a certain day, a strange and wonderful thing happens. Once I have written these things down, I am then, in a sense, a slave to what I have written. The written word has magic to it. Every time I see the unaccomplished items on that list my conscience will tingle and a red light will go on. And every time I cross one off, I get a tiny little feeling of "Me Tarzan. I did it again!" I am caricaturing, but after all, if we can constantly give ourselves a series of little pats on the back, if we are on the receiving end of a lot of self-validating tricks, how wonderful life can be.

I think a device such as this is an absolute necessity — especially now, when you are making a change, when you are exploring a new territory. It can be useful in logging your personal objectives — your weight loss, for example — as well as your daily appointments and accomplishments.

Let me mention two other considerations in the preparation for your market campaign. First, it is very important to be dressed as well as is consistent with your personality, your own particular grace. You probably know the kind of clothes you look well in; if you are in doubt about it, or about the appropriateness of what you are considering wearing to an interview, get advice from friends or family. I am not suggesting that you invest hundreds of dollars in your wardrobe, of course — but cast a meticulous eye upon it. Confidence that you are well dressed is an important factor in your general attitude about yourself, and it will show.

The second point involves meticulousness of another sort — in matters of courtesy. Courteous acts play such a vital part in the pursuit of your career as well as in your personal relationships that they are stressed in connection with almost every subject treated in this book. In a rough-and-ready world all of us tend to drop some of the little courtesies, and as you get yourself in trim in other ways you can also set about restoring lapsed habits of courteous behavior. Courtesy, like charity, begins at home.

When you are thoughtlessly discourteous you do yourself a grave disservice. Let me give you an example from real life. I am the president of a firm. Outside my office, in an office of her own, sits my secretary — my personal assistant. She is modest; she does not put on any airs; she works hard and she holds an important position. Suppose, when you come in for an appointment with me, she does not impress you very much and you make some wisecrack, some brash little comment. She does not like it but she does not say a word. Instead, she smiles and you forget the incident.

You come into my office and have a perfectly nice interview with me and we set up another, When you leave, my secretary comes in and I tell her about the new appointment.

"Hmm," she says. "Is he coming back? I thought he was ill-mannered." And you are dead.

The president who cuts you off his list is not protecting his secretary. He is protecting his own dignity. Who insults my secretary insults me. She is under the shield of my power. This is literally true.

And it works both ways. I once interviewed a job applicant who was wonderfully polite and obviously capable but a little too high-powered for the job I needed to fill. He was courteous and wrote me a beautiful thank-you letter. A few days later, the switchboard operator said to me, "Mr. Djeddah, what a wonderful man that Mr. So-and-So is. Do you know he actually thanked me for the courtesy I had shown him in putting him through to you? Wasn't that nice?"

That man had a job with me within six months. Little causes can trigger big effects.

Now that you are physically fit, mentally alert, spiritually sound, purposeful, nicely organized, pleasantly dressed, courteous, and on the threshold of getting down to your campaign in earnest, let's go back to the subject of focus again.

In going out into the job market, you start when you know exactly what you are looking for. You should be armed with a résumé focused on what you are after. It is never wise to go into the market as a utility man. Even though you have the ability to do many things, it is a very poor method of getting a job. To go into the market unfocused in the hope that if you are available for everything — anything — some kindly angel will suggest a job is not helpful. Repeat: It is a very poor method of getting a job.

Let me give you some examples of the role that focus plays. The first involves a blunder out of my past. A man came into my office one day and said, "I'm so happy that you people have opened an office here. I really should have visited your office in Boston. I worked there three or four years."

"Delighted to meet you," I said. "What's your problem?"

"Oh, I don't have any problem. I'm working with the FRD Corporation, and I'm as safe as can be. But, you know, I thought that at this time of my life — age thirty-nine, wife and six children, two cars and all the rest — that this is a time to think about getting ahead."

Now, I digress to say that it took many, many years of counseling work for me to discover that no one ever really comes in simply to "get ahead." It is never true. It is like going to the doctor without a symptom.

"What's wrong?" the doctor asks.

"Wrong, Doctor? Why, nothing. I'm perfectly healthy."

"Then why are you here?"

"I want to be healthier, Doctor."

That never happens. What does happen is that if I have a stomachache, I go to the doctor and tell him what is troubling me. And while I am there, I say, "Examine my heart and my kidneys and everything else. I want to improve everything now so this doesn't happen again."

Back to the man who wanted to "get ahead." He was a bright man, brilliant really. And he was doing rather well for his area — making about $30,000. He said, "There is no hurry. I can afford to look around."

So we defined a job for him which was purely hypothetical and speculative, a kind of dream job which would utilize his talents and bring in high rewards. We both knew this was theoretical. We agreed that if his circumstances altered we would have to crash down to reality in a hurry.

Eight weeks after he became a client, he came in and said, "Well, it's happened."

"What's happened?"

"They fired me."

"That's amazing," I said. "I thought you were as safe as could be." Of course, he was not; when he came in the first time, he came in doubt. "Well, we've got to get busy and redo your résumé realistically. This is where we start a real market campaign."

"Don't be silly," he said. "Look, they gave me three months' severance pay. I've got time now to go out and try for the job we've already designed. I'm going for the long shot. I'm going to speculate."

I am sorry to say that this sounded reasonable to me at the time; I was not knowledgeable enough then to see what a mistake it was. It was very unreasonable, because that man went out with no clear focus. He had three months' pay in his pocket and dreams of an unrealistic job in his head. Two months later he came back. He had had thirty or forty interviews and great bunches of no interest. He was crushed morally and emotionally— shattered. And he was Pavlov-reflexed for failure. Every time he went to an interview, he expected a big fat "No" and that is what he got. It was only after we were able to refocus him and reconstruct him, put the fragments together, that he was able to solve his problem.

The second example, too dismal to linger over, involves a case we had a few years ago—a man who went to ninety interviews without getting an offer of a job. When he talked to us, this man always agreed on a plan of action, but as soon as he got out of the door he said to himself, "I really don't agree with their thinking. I'm available for anything. I'm not going to limit my market." He did not limit his market, so he had no market.

Let us suppose you are hiring a sales representative. Two people come in to see you. One is brilliant and you say, "What do you want to do?" And he replies, "Oh, I can do just about anything. What have you got?" So you think, "Gee, this guy's brilliant but he's unstable. He doesn't really know what he wants to do. Tomorrow, if I give him this job as a salesman, he might go flirting down a different alley. I don't think he's the person I want."

Then a relatively stupid candidate comes along: nicely dressed, very polite. You ask, "What do you want to do?" and she says, "I want to sell." So you are very shrewd and you say, "We have a job in quality control."

The candidate looks up and says, "Quality control? What's that?" You explain and she says, "Gee, I don't see how that could lead me into selling." So the interview continues and the candidate makes her point: "I want to sell. I want to sell." She is very likely to get the job—even though she is not brilliant— because she knows who she is and what she wants to do.

When you are properly in focus, you should be able to answer the question "What do I want to do?" with five or six succinct statements of your purpose and goal. The question will be asked and it is well to be prepared for it — in the full knowledge of your capabilities.

4 Seven Rules to Protect Your Campaign

Now you are focused. How do you start looking for a position? Before you start, I am going to give you seven rules to guide you in the market campaign. With regard to these rules I make this comment: they are designed for your protection, your self-preservation. As you will see, some are rules for navigating in unknown waters, for the time when you feel you haven't quite got your bearings in a strange situation. When you are perfectly at ease, you may drop some of the roles and give your personality full rein.

The seven rules which guide your market campaign

1. Never take short cuts.
2. Preserve your dignity at all times.
3. Do not let anyone do anything for you that you would not do yourself.
4. Take the burden of action into your own hands whenever possible.
5. Keep quiet if you cannot be constructive.

6. Do not reveal your salary or the salary you want until you have been offered a job.
7. Never accept or reject an offer while in the room with the interviewer.

The first rule of your market campaign is: *Never take short cuts.* This is a matter of common sense, as you will see. You must go through all the rituals that will be revealed as we go along without short-cutting them.

I will anticipate some later material and give you an example of a short cut. As a procedure, we tell each client, before an interview, that the interviewer must be in possession of a résumé at least a day ahead. But the client thinks, "This can't apply to Jones down the street. I've known her ten years. She was my boss." So he calls Ms. Jones without letting her see a résumé. That is short-cutting. It is very dangerous.

It is dangerous because nobody knows you. Not really. Your own boss does not know you. He is too concerned with other things. You know a surgeon down the street. You play golf with him. You have drinks with him and joke with him. And then one day, you see this man in his terrifying white mask, his white overalls, with his knives and other instruments of horror, about to operate. And you realize you do not know him. You have never seen this side of your friend. You know only one or two aspects of him. Therefore, to meet someone who is uninformed about you actually is to prevent him from performing.

A friend comes to you and says, "I have a very complicated problem and I'd like your advice." Naturally you want to help. But when he throws his complicated problem at you, he has caught you unprepared; all he can get is short-order cooking. At best, you are going to be able to give him 20 percent of what you could have given if he had warned you of the problem two days before and let you have time to think about it.

So, in general, you must not short-cut. The only kind of short cut permitted is the elimination of a formal letter to a friend. You can call him on the telephone two or three days ahead and tell him you want to arrange an appointment with him. Then, when the appointment is set, tell him you are going to send him something about you to read.

Follow the rituals. That is the safest, surest course. Many times, the more creative of my clients refuse to follow the rules—they would rather try a few ideas of their own. This is sometimes a waste of time, but even as they wander off the recommended path, they have a floor under them. They know they can always fall back on the rules given here—and they usually do.

The second rule of your market campaign is: *Preserve your dignity.* You do not want to make your rounds as if you are trying to sell leprosy. You will trade with people, but you will not ask favors. Whom will you meet? In the public area of the market, you are going to approach people who may have arranged interviews through an agency or an ad or a confetti letter (see Chapter 6). In none of those cases are you asking for any favors. They are out to public tender, and you are one of the people who bid; you are at the interview in response to their call.

But in the main area of the market, you will be meeting people from whom you want advice, although they will be aware that you are looking for a job. What will someone's attitude be when asked for advice? Generally, advice is given with pleasure. And it is a fair trade. If you ask for help and you get good advice, you feel happy and enriched. In return, you have helped your advisor feel good and happy to have been able to help. So you both gain. It is a fair trade.

You may meet specialized situations in which the interviewers try to trick you into revealing personal traits, weaknesses, temper, or nervousness. There is one rule that saves you from all of them: You are going to walk into any room as a free, independent American citizen demanding for yourself the courtesy you grant to everyone else. You do not have to put up with any tricks and you will not.

The third rule of your market campaign is: *Do not let anyone do anything for you that you would not do yourself.* This rule may be difficult to apply. Let me give you an example. You are looking for a position and come in to see me for advice and, possibly, a job. I say, "Look here, why don't you leave me six of your résumés. I'll see that the right people get them." What do you say? It is difficult to say, "No. You can't have copies of my résumé," and repulse a friendly offer.

But if you give me copies of your résumé you will be doing the very thing you would not do yourself: You are going to let me short-cut things for you—thereby breaking Rule Number One. Because if I have your résumés, I will go to six people and say, "I know this guy. He's good. Do you have a job for him?"

That is the last way in the world you can get a job, and it will kill six good contacts for you. So with due decorum and decency, you say, "I appreciate the thought and I want to use your help, but perhaps we can do it differently. I'd really like to chat with these people myself. I'd be delighted if you could set up the appointments for me."

The fourth rule of your market campaign is: *Take the burden of action into your own hands whenever possible.* When you are in a room with a man, he is under all the impact of your courtesy, your charm, and your ability, and he wants to perform at his top level and be really nice to you. Say you are seeking advice from a high-level executive. At a certain point he says, "I really don't know whom I can suggest to you. Give me a couple of days to think about it."

Do you thank him and walk away? No. You could say, very politely, something like this: "I appreciate your taking the time to see me. May I call you in a day or so?" He has asked for a couple of days to think about your problem. He is not likely to say you cannot call. This keeps the action in your hands.

If you do not take the action into your own hands—if you leave it up to the executive who wants a couple of days to think things over, you most likely will be forgotten. He says, "I'll get back to you in a few days," and then his tax bill comes in, his son wrecks the family car, his boss asks him for a rush report, and fifty other problems come across his desk. He is not sufficiently concerned about you to remember his promise to call. Once he forgets, you have lost him.

I will tell you why. If he should be reminded — somehow — that he did not call you back, he is likely to rationalize: "I'm not really that interested. I forgot, but it really doesn't matter." Very few people are big enough to call up and apologize — and admit they have forgotten. When you are with him in the room, he is on your side; he is interested in you. That is the time to take action into your own hands to ensure a further meeting.

Question: *Isn't there a danger that this will seem pushy?*

Answer: *That depends on the way you say it and on your attitude. Attitudes are conveyed by many nonverbal means. If you are pushy, you will look and sound pushy. If you are not pushy, you can take the action into your own hands.*

The fifth rule of your market campaign is: *Keep quiet if you cannot be constructive.* This is very important. In all your interviews, if you cannot be constructive, keep your mouth closed. Somebody says to you, "You don't have any experience managing an office of thirty-six people because up to now you've managed an office with only thirty-five people in it." Do not start a long dissertation on the question. You can answer, "There's not much difference, really, between thirty-five and thirty-six. I always felt four percent underworked when I was managing thirty-five people." That is constructive.

Do not fall into a negative frame of mind and agree with your interviewer that you cannot do some job. We all ignore the fact that we often think out loud. And we all ignore the fact that other people do too. As an employer, I could say, "Well, you've never sold banana leaves before and I really think that takes a lot of experience." That may be me thinking aloud to myself, questioning myself. And if you come back at me with "Well, that's right. I've never sold banana leaves. Perhaps I should test myself first by selling fig leaves," you are being negative. If you cannot be constructive and positive, you must always be silent.

The sixth rule of your market campaign is: *Do not reveal your salary or the salary you want until you have been offered a job.* Any time you make a statement about the salary you expect you have lost two-thirds of your market. You are bound to be either too high or too low or in the middle — on the nose — but the odds against being on the nose are two-to-one against. Not very good odds.

Let us say you are being interviewed and are asked how much you are making. You say you are making or want to make $25,000. Now she has two others working in the department into which she would like to fit you. They each make $27,000, and the job she has in mind for you carries a salary of $30,000. So she says to herself, "That's a shame, not quite the caliber I'm looking for." That might be completely wrong, but you have lost out because you were truthful and the figure you suggested was too low. Nobody who sees an automobile priced at $8,000 gives $10,000 for it. If the car were marked at $8,000 it might go for $7,800, but it is not going to bring $10,800.

There are many legitimate ways of evading a direct question about salary, ways which later will be discussed at length. Here let me illustrate just one element that lies in the question "How much are you making?" or "How much do you want?"

I once had a problem with a secretary. She was a very effective personal assistant except for one curious flaw. She took the preliminary information on clients, but when she brought back the sheets they never included ages. This was very aggravating, and I spoke to her about it a number of times.

"Get the person's age."

"Yes, sir."

The next client came in. No age. I spoke to the girl again.

"I'll take care of it," she said.

Four, five, six more times, and no ages. So I called her in and said, "Nan, I am getting frustrated. Next time I get a preliminary sheet without the man's age, I'm going to fire you, release you, make you vanish, cause you to nonexist on the premises, to cease earning money with this firm. Do you understand?"

"Oh, yes, sir."

Sure enough, the next preliminary sheet she handed me did not have the man's age noted. Tears in her eyes.

"I don't know why I can't do it," Nan said. "I promise to get the age and I always forget. I can't do it."

This happened with two girls who followed Nan. So I said to myself, "I am on the verge of a great discovery, a truth about human nature." It is this: Anything that has an emotional connotation places us on an emotional level. Now, emotionally, we are all, at the most, four years old. And when you are four years old, anything you do gives me the right to do the same. You pinch me; it is my turn to pinch you. Little children have reciprocal rights. So if I ask your age—an emotion-laden question—you have the reciprocal right to ask mine. If I don't want you to know my age, I will never ask yours.

What has this got to do with salary? Well, when I ask about your salary, I know I'm cheating. If you don't blurt it out right away, I would never dare ask the question again because I have the horrible, uncomfortable feeling that you are entitled, emotionally, to ask in return, "How much do *you* make?"

The seventh rule of your market campaign is: *Never accept or reject an offer while in the room with the interviewer.* Let me cite an example of why you should not accept or reject any offer on the spot. We had a client with an MBA from Columbia, a bright boy. He lost a position in Hartford, Connecticut, and came to Boston to start a market campaign. His first interview was with the head of a well-known New England firm. The executive interviewed our client for three hours and then offered him the ideal job, absolutely ideal. And then he said, "The salary will be seventeen thousand."

That was six or seven thousand less than the man was worth. So our client, remembering the rules, came back to us.

"What do I do now? He offered me the perfect job, but the salary is too low."

"Keep moving," I said. "When you get another offer, come to me."

He did get another offer—for $25,000. And he came in to see me.

"How do the two jobs compare, regardless of the money?" I asked.

"The first job is ideal," he said. "That man tailored a job for me. He photographed my soul and offered me an image."

So I said, "Go back to the first man and ask him for advice. Tell him how you feel about the job he has offered, and see if he thinks there is any way the salary can be adjusted."

The executive heard our client out and said, "Let me think about it for a day or two."

The next day he called. "I have some very exciting news for you. We have a new position open." Then he put a new title on the exact job he had described in the beginning. But this time the salary was $19,500.

The client came back to us. "What do I do?"

"Keep going," I said.

The ABG Corporation offered him $32,000, and I sent him back to the first firm. He showed the executive there the $32,000 offer in writing and the man said, "Let me think about it."

Two days later, the executive called again. "You're fortunate," he said. "An entirely new situation has emerged." Then he described the original job—the identical job—but now it had another title and a new salary, $24,500. "You've got two hours to make up your mind," he added.

The client accepted the position at $24,500, a wise decision because the job was exactly right for him. In effect, the whole thing had been a testing process. But notice the point—it had all started at $17,000. We have seen offers start at $20,000 and go all the way to $30,000. In one such case the client refused the job because he said he could not trust the man offering it. I believe he was right. But he did not reject the offer while he was being interviewed. We discussed it before he turned it down.

Do not reject any offer while being interviewed; do not accept any offer while being interviewed. There will be examples of good and bad use of this rule later on.

The rules of your market campaign are only for use in areas where you feel unfamiliar. Except for the three or four there for your own self-preservation, they are only for the early stages. When you are in empathy with your interviewer, when you are on the right footing, you will be guided by your own personality.

If you are hard sell, you will be hard sell. If you are soft sell, you will be soft sell. If you are medium sell, you will be medium sell. We do not teach birds to fly. All that we teach in technique is merely for the period of the interview when you feel uncomfortable. When you are yourself, you need no other support at all. And the supports are there to lead you to be yourself. How could it help you to sell something that was different from yourself? It would be worse than useless.

To summarize:

- Never take short cuts.
- Preserve your dignity.
- Do not let anyone do things for you.
- Try to take the burden of the action.
- Keep quiet if you cannot be constructive.
- Do not discuss salary before a job is offered.
- Never accept or reject an offer on the spot.

There is another rule: Thank-you letters must be sent to everyone who has been helpful. I will discuss this in **Chapters 7** and 9.

5 Nine Ways to Find a Job

Now that you're ready with the seven rules, how do you get to use them? In other words, where are the jobs? Your market can be divided into two parts: the *published and the unpublished*.

The published section consists of jobs you read about in newspapers, jobs which can be had through employment agencies or recruiters, and jobs which may be revealed to you by a mail campaign. These areas probably add up to about 20 percent of the market.

Although percentages fluctuate according to time and geographical location, as a rule of thumb, 5 percent of the jobs with salaries from $15,000 and up are filled by employment agencies. (The agency figure drops to 2 percent for jobs over $30,000, while major consulting and recruiting firms account for placement of 2 percent in this category.) Newspaper ads represent 7 to 8 percent of the jobs available, and state and federal employment agencies fill 3 to 5 percent. The government, including the military, provides 7 to 8 percent of the jobs. Confetti letters (see Chapter 6) fill 3 to 5 percent.

The unpublished section represents about 80 percent of the market, up to about the $50,000 salary level. Above that, 90 percent of the jobs available are unpublished. At the $100,000 level, almost 100 percent are unpublished. Jobs in the unpublished market are given to people in a key executive's room — the offices of presidents, vice presidents, or department heads in large firms.

In the unpublished area of your market about half of the 80 percent are potential *jobs and not* current *jobs.* This is most important for you to understand.

But potential jobs can be created, and the created job is the prime job, because you build it with the man who is going to employ you. You do not have any competition, because you will be evaluated in relation to specific problems — not in comparison with other people. No salary or other conditions have been preset. They are open to negotiation — depending exactly on how much your prospective employer thinks you are worth.

Before we set out to do anything at all, we want to make sure that every step is a successful step because we want to be Pavlov-reflexed for success. Nothing brings success like success. If you know you can take positive action and that this action will be successful, you will not only have a pleasant market campaign — you will also have a successful market campaign.

Is there a way to guarantee success? There is. If your objectives are reasonable you can most assuredly attain them.

There are only twelve ways in the whole world to get a job. Some of them are not very good, but I will include them all in this book — nine in this chapter — for the sake of completeness.

But, before we consider them, let me cite a few mechanical aids you will need for your market campaign which will make your course simpler and more effective than it might be otherwise.

Letters. Your market campaign will be tied together with letters. Several examples are given in this book. Do not follow them slavishly; they are not designed for that. Change the wording to suit your own vocabulary, approach and style while maintaining the purpose of the letter. You can write better letters than my examples and you should. Briefness counts.

Do not use the business stationery of the firm where you are currently employed—that is, not unless you are its president. If you haven't your own personal stationery, get some. A letter with your name and address imprinted at the top looks better and is more impressive than a letter written on plain white paper. There are firms which turn out stationery which has the look and feel of engraving, and many other companies which produce attractive printed stationery. I think it is all right to go into dignified pastel colors if you prefer—a light blue, green, or gray.

Thank-you's. Everyone you deal with must get a thank-you note. It is not necessary to type them all. Where an interview is not going to bring about further progress, it is proper and courteous to use a small preprinted thank-you card—these are available in any stationery store—with a short handwritten note on it.

Campaign Sheets. You must keep a record of your interviews, the time spent on each one and how you came to get it. Examples of such sheets are given in Chapter 15.

Now for the ways to get a job.

Number 1: Almost Worthless

The first way to get a job is the door-to-door approach. You go to the library and list the names of every firm which could possibly have the kind of job you want. "This is a logical move," you reason, "because my market is necessarily among the firms which can give me a job."

So you come up with a list of four hundred firms, put on a pair of shoes with thick soles, and start to work your way down the list. After several weeks of the most laborious work, you almost certainly will not have found a job—although when you got to the tenth firm you heard they had just given exactly the job you wanted to another man, a week or so before, and when you were at the sixty-sixth, "your" job was open at the ninety-seventh, which of course you could not get to in time.

What I am highlighting here is that if you proceed in this manner you might go without finding a job for years before your arrival coincided with a job opening. So, in one sense, a market campaign is a time equation: you must solve it so that you arrive when and where the job emerges. The knock-on-the-door approach is a disastrous one. I actually saw a man in Boston who had been on 133 interviews on the knock-on-every-door basis — with no results. Someone might possibly hire you if he was under pressure — if he was hauling coal and needed an extra pair of arms. But for anything more sophisticated you will not be hired. Reflect a moment — would you hire someone who knocked on the door and asked for a job? He probably would never get by the receptionist in the outer office, and certainly he would not get by your secretary. Yet this approach, silly as it is, still exists.

Number 2: Special Situations

The second approach has some value in very special situations. This is to sell an idea or a bunch of ideas — and to sell yourself with them. This approach covers a very small area of the market and is open only to very imaginative people, inventors or specialists in certain areas.

Here is an example of how a man had an idea and sold his services. This man worked for a large company with divisions and laboratories in several cities. His own division started with much promise but dwindled away because the product it was supposed to make and sell was too expensive. Higher authority decided to drop the effort, and our man, who was very competent and bright, sat at his desk frustrated and idle.

As his frustrations grew, he began to think, "I'd like to live on the West Coast, and there must be many companies like this one with innumerable divisions and innumerable duplications of effort. The government frequently orders research and development on many items which are later dropped. Patents pile up on shelves. What is needed is a central department whose function would be to examine and compare research and development in all areas of the company — to avoid duplication of effort and to discover products in one division which could be marketed in others or licensed to another company that could be interested in their manufacture. In other words, a department that could find out what goes on in an overall way."

So this clever fellow sat down and wrote letters to the presidents of several companies suggesting that they must already have such a department and suggesting also that he had the technical knowledge and the ability for the diplomatic negotiations required to handle it. The companies to whom he addressed himself did not, of course, have such a department, but they recognized the shrewdness of his idea. Several presidents called him in, mainly to pick his brains. In the end, he was given a position to set up such a department for a company on the West Coast, and his objective was achieved: he was at work on the West Coast.

That is the second—and limited—way to get a job—by selling yourself along with a patent or an idea.

Number 3: Buy a Business

The third way to get a job is to buy a business of your own. Quite probably, one hundred out of every hundred people want to go into business for themselves. Of the 70 percent who admit it, about 30 percent try it at one time or another. Of these, only 4 percent survive. You must proceed with the greatest care in this area.

Number 4: "Wonderful Me"

A fourth way to get a job is to go to the newspapers and advertise yourself—to announce that wonderful you is available. This approach is ludicrous because it ignores the very basis on which personnel advertising is published. Firms that advertise for personnel are selling—they are looking for people who come to them as a result of their ads. They do not read the ads to buy.

You will, however, get three or four answers to your ad: two from insurance companies and one from an employment agency which, once it has read your ad, knows it can do the job better than you.

Naturally, there are exceptions to this generally fruitless method. If you are a specialist in some line, it could well be of value to place ads in specialized trade magazines. Here you are dealing with a select public. If you are a hi-fi treble-audio specialist, advertise in the hi-fi treble-audio magazines and someone may be interested in your proposal. The cost is small.

Number 5: Government Job

There is, of course, a market which should not be ignored. Outside of marriage it is the biggest one in the world—federal, state, and local governments with all their endless ramifications. The approach to this market—unless the position is based on competitive examinations—consists of two alternatives. First is a predetermined form with which no one can help you—an application form on which you list a full chronology of your career, with no omissions or dressing up to sharpen focus, because there are laws against perjury. Applications to government posts *can* be made more effective by the second alternative: personal referral. Briefly stated, if a high government official can be convinced you are the right applicant for a job, you will be hired. No one should forget that government is a very, very large employer—7 or 8 percent of the entire market. The first steps toward government employment are set and mechanical, but if need be, other legitimate steps can be taken, which are no different from those discussed in the second half of the book, in connection with the unpublished section of the private job market.

Number 6: Employment Agencies

Another way of getting a job is to go to an employment agency, which will set up interviews for you. Employment agencies cover about five jobs out of every hundred at around $15,000-a-year level, or about 5 percent. As the curve of the salary rises that percentage dips, and when the offered salary is $30,000 the percentage handled by employment agencies is quite low.

The agency charges a fee for its services, which may be paid either by you or the hiring company. These fees can be a high item of cost to the employer, ranging anywhere from 10 to 20 percent of the first year's salary. This fact, especially in smaller companies, is taken into account in fixing the starting salary. To put it another way: it is always the job candidate who pays the fee, whether he is aware of it or not.

Since your average association with a firm lasts over four years and the agency fee is tax deductible, it would be wise for you to arrange to pay the fee yourself. For instance, if the salary is $30,000 and the fee is $6,000 and you negotiate the starting salary to $32,500 and pay the fee, you will lose $6,000 and gain back $2,500 × 4, or $10,000, for a net profit of $4,000 spread over the first four years.

One additional point about agencies: your selection of which to register with may be made on the basis of an attractive ad in the newspaper under an agency's name. You should know that not infrequently the job advertised is fictitious. The purpose of such ads is to enable the agency to obtain leads for their files of qualified candidates. (The same dubious procedure has been used from time to time by some counseling firms to get leads for potential fee-paying clients.)

Number 7: Recruiters

Now we come to a more sophisticated area, the executive search firm, the recruiting firms—the seventh way to find a job. These services cover about 2 percent of the market—two jobs out of every hundred.

Originally these firms were used only for hiring the rare bird. A company would come to them and say, "We need a specialist who knows all about resetting the kneecaps of fleas." And the recruiter would say, "Well, we know one man of that kind who is very busy on the fleas of the Congo, but we think we can buy him away from Schweitzer's organization and bring him home for you. Of course, it will be expensive."

The important thing to know about recruiters and executive searchers is this: No one out of work should ever bother to register with them. Why? Very simple. These people do not know how to select anyone for a job. (In this respect they are not exceptional; almost no one knows how to select anyone for a job—80 percent of all workers are in the wrong job.) The body snatchers are interested only in someone who is employed. They will take the general manager of a certain corporation *because* that is who he is—he has the validity of his job—and their clients will be very pleased to get someone so "competent." But the recruiters certainly will not take on an unknown wanderer from the sidewalk, for who knows what may be wrong with him?

To get in touch with employment agencies, executive recruiters, and management consultants, typed letters should be prepared along the following lines:

Dear Sir or Madam:

Your clients frequently are in the market for qualified people with my background. I would welcome the opportunity to be interviewed by any interested parties.

You will understand the need to treat both this letter and the accompanying résumé as confidential. My present employer should not be contacted at this time.

Yours truly,

Résumé enclosed

No one will ever check with your employer, but the last sentence emphasizes in a subtle manner that you are not being fired and are perfectly secure.

Number 8: Management Consultants

Still another way of finding a position is to register with management consulting firms, which also cover about 2 percent of the market. Quite often they are asked to staff or restaff certain parts of a company they have revamped, and it can do no harm if they know of your availability. This approach is usually ineffectual, however, if you are unemployed.

Number 9: Newspaper Ads

We have now gone through eight ways of getting a job. The ninth way is to answer a newspaper advertisement. Jobs offered in newspapers cover about 7 to 8 percent of the job market.

There are situations here that you should be aware of. Pick up a Sunday paper — 75 cents' worth of news features, comics, columnists, and classified ads. The Sunday paper is a universal affair. Anyone with change in his pocket can buy one and dream — widows, jailbirds, schoolboys, retired Army officers, upholsterer's apprentices, taxi drivers, gym teachers, and unfrocked FBI men. You and I and all the rest see an ad — an ad, let us say, asking for a general manager of the Very Strong Paper Carton Company at $30,000 a year. That advertisement is going to be answered by hundreds of dreamers.

You and I are not dreamers. Let us look at that advertisement together. It may well not mean what it says. Here is why. If I wanted a manager at $30,000, wouldn't I be foolish to advertise the fact? Indeed I would, because I would attract all the ambitious people at the $15,000 and $18,000 levels who very much want to rise to the pleasant neighborhood of $30,000. But I also want $1.05 for my money — not 75 cents' worth — so I would take great care with my ad. I would not advertise for a $30,000 manager — I would advertise for a manager and deliberately give the impression that the job was worth more than it is; I would advertise the job as worth "up to $35,000" with the "up to" in very small type. Most people would never even read the "up to." I would word my ad in that way because I want all the real $30,000 types and know that I may even catch a few naive $35,000 types who still believe what they read. I would get value for my advertising money, because the ad will get far more answers than I would normally get — there is a $1.05 return for my advertising dollar.

My ad for a position "up to $35,000" in the *New York Times* or the *Wall Street Journal* would bring in hundreds — in some cases thousands — of answers depending on the broadness of the definition of the job. The number of answers diminishes as the specifications become more definite. Thus if I advertised for a

PhD in mathematics with emphasis on the theory of numbers, I would get fewer answers than if I called for a general manager who was dynamic, who had an MBA and was a money producer. An ad like the second would bring in perhaps a thousand answers.

That is a great many answers — and these answers are never read by anybody in a responsible position. Think a minute: the time to read them and analyze them would be almost fantastic. There is no computer on the market which can compare the variables that appear in five hundred letters, let alone three thousand. So if you want your answer to the ad to be read and favorably reviewed, you have to resort to art rather than science.

Who does read the letters? Not the person who will decide on the candidate and could therefore be presumed to understand what you're talking about. Not even the personnel manager — not unless you pass the first big hurdle. No, the letters are read by an assistant of some sort whose dedication to the job is low priority. The assistant divides the letters into two piles — the good and the no-good. The good pile finally ends up containing about 10 percent of the replies, which are turned over to the personnel department, and the screening job continues. Finally, about forty letters are left. From that, personnel selects about ten and calls the writers in for interviews. From the interviews, one applicant is hired — a perfectly valid person for the job. But what happened to the hundreds of other perfectly valid people who were not even called? What are the approaches to make sure you get an interview?

The first approach is the form of your answer. Your natural reaction — it is everyone's natural reaction — is to announce yourself as something special, to impress the individual who has the job to award. So you send a long, involved description of your brilliance and amazing management talent. The aforementioned assistant picks it up and says, "This person sounds like an acrobat. He can do everything. He sounds like an idiot." And your letter goes in the no-good piles, simply because he does not understand what you are talking about.

You must answer the ad as though you are writing for a child of six. No slur intended. It is simply a realistic recognition of the circumstances. It also applies to *any* letter you write that is accompanied by your résumé. Your résumé is a good one; it is a portrait of you, properly focused. Your accompanying letter is confined to the minimum message: "you ask for A, B, and C. I have A, B, and C. You will see from the enclosed résumé that I also have X, Y, and Z, and I want an interview."

Simplicity of form is the first condition for answering any ad. Complexity will almost certainly put your letter in the no-good pile.

Since the problem is really a mathematical one, would it not be wise to offer a mathematical solution? Multiply the number of your answers. Type out two or three copies of your letter. Send along the original with your résumé. Then, in a day or so, send another, marked "copy." On the third day, send out another "copy." Résumés should accompany these letters, too. If you had a 25 percent chance of having your letter favorably read because of its simplicity, you now have a 75 percent chance of getting into the good pile. If you are in the good pile, your chances of getting to an interview are ten times better than anyone else's—because your résumé is bound to impress the personnel department.

Another way to get special attention is to certify or register your letter. A registered letter is something special. It produces a twinge of anxiety when it comes into an office. Is Uncle Sam after me for that $200 deduction? Is my wife writing to say all has been discovered? Is it a letter from someone who slipped on the front steps of the building and is about to sue for $500,000? Your letter will be read.

This is another aspect of this part of the published market. There are two categories of ads: the ads which appear under a box number and the ads which appear under a company name.

These are discussed in the next chapter, but here let me make a comment about all advertisements, regardless of whether they are box-numbered or issued under a company name. Eighty percent of the jobs offered in the ads are filled by candidates who do not have the qualifications described in the advertisement. The ads call for an engineer, a mechanical engineer with five years' experience in hydraulic pumps, and they hire an electrical engineer with three months' experience.

People give a description of what they think they want. Someone in personnel takes out an old government book, reads a description of the job, and puts that in the paper. This gives you an advantage—you can read all the ads with your tongue in cheek. If you feel you can do the job advertised, answer the ad regardless of what the advertiser says he wants, whether he says he wants a PhD no more than thirty-nine years old, or a manager who must have five years' experience, or whatever. If you feel certain you could do the job, answer the ad, because the chances are one out of two that they will hire someone with no prior experience, and the chances are eight out of ten that they will hire someone with qualifications different from the ones they advertised.

I promised twelve ways to get a job. Three to go. Read on.

6 Letters to Write—
and Method Number Ten

Before leaving Number 9, Newspaper Ads, let us consider box-numbered ads. Box-numbered ads are often inserted in the paper by small or doubtful operators. They may even be put into the paper by people who have no jobs to offer—they are looking for lists of certain specified people to whom they will send mailings of one sort or another later on. Ads may also be used purely for promotional reasons. Some companies advertise for engineers or scientists or chemists to work on research on the rare metal fleebite. They may get a few answers from people who have knowledge of the rare metal fleebite—but they also remind countless others that fleebite is available, and their business takes an upward bounce.

Though box-numbered ads are suspect, they are nevertheless sometimes irresistible. They outline jobs which sound ideal, the perfect job for you. It is too much for flesh and blood to endure, so you dash off an answer. If you must answer, go ahead, but do it in the way suggested in this chapter: multiply your chances of getting an interview. It is the surest approach.

Of the newspaper ads in which the company name appears, there are two categories. One is the ad sponsored by an important functional executive — a plant manager, a director of research, or a vice president — in which event, your surest bet is to certify or register your letter — written simply — to the person named in the ad.

Alternatively, the ad may be sponsored by someone who is not in a key executive position. If the ad is sponsored by an important person, you will write directly to the person named. If the ad is sponsored by a person whose title indicates he or she is small potatoes, prepare to write two letters. First you zero in on the company at a higher level. Find the name of the proper executive — president, vice-president — from business directories in your library and, if you are unemployed, write a letter similar to this:

Dear Mr. Bowen:

You will notice from the attached notes that I have the qualifications required for the position described in your advertisement.

I hold myself available for an interview at your convenience.

Please treat my application confidentially at this time.

Yours truly,

Then, a day or two later, write the same letter again, addressing it this time to the man named in the ad. If the top executive, Mr. Bowen, simply routes your letter to Mr. Small Potatoes as a matter of course, Mr. S. P. has double exposure to you, and one of them bears Mr. Bowen's handwritten "refer to" mark.

If you are employed, you send Mr. Bowen the following letter:

Dear Mr. Bowen:

Although I am employed as —————at the XYZ Corporation, I have confidentially decided to make a change. The accompanying notes illustrate my purposes and qualifications.

I am genuinely interested in joining your firm.

With a view to acquainting you with what I have to offer, I will call your office in the next few days to arrange for an appointment at your convenience.

Sincerely yours,

You follow this one up, a day or two later, with a letter identical to my first "Mr. Bowen" example, addressed to Mr. S. P. In all cases you enclose your résumé.

It should be noted that in very large corporations, where procedures are rigidly observed, this double-barreled way of answering an ad is not particularly useful. But in smaller companies Mr. Bowen may get directly in touch with you. Why? Well, eighty-five times out of a hundred he came from the sales force and ninety-nine times out of a hundred he feels unloved; top executives almost always feel insecure. Such a man is at the top because his insecurity drove him to work harder and compete more vigorously to justify his existence—and, in turn, he is insecure at the top because of his isolation. The selection of key personnel (you) by the top man himself gives him the (endlessly disappointed) hope of finally being able to hire perfect communicators who will loyally espouse his point of view. Furthermore, the insecure man at the top needs constant proof of his validity and ability, and the biggest proof is the inefficiency of others. He hardly dares take a vacation because his company could not get along without him. When he does go on a vacation he returns, sees all the mistakes that have been made, and points out all the negatives to all hands. This makes him feel valid—the validation of criticism, a narcotic very few of us can live without.

Under these circumstances, Mr. Bowen very likely will ask you to meet with him and, if you are right for the job in question, he will hire you. This gives him another opportunity to validate his existence. He will say wearily, "If it were not for me, you would still be looking around for the right person. But I've saved you once again. Once again, I've pulled the rabbit out of the hat and found the person we need."

Please do not think this is a fairy tale. It happens every day.

Let me tell you a true story—a classic case, but still true. When I was in my counseling firm's Boston office, Mr. X came in to see us.

"I am working for my uncle, who manufactures soup," he said. "I am paid nine thousand a year and for this I must bow to the east, the west, the north, and the south each and every day, and every day I have to thank my ancient gods that my uncle manufactures soup. He reminds me in every one of the fourteen hours I work, six days of every week, what a lucky boy I am. I need help. Can you help me?"

We went to work with him, but he was an almost impossible case because, with his job taking eighty-four hours a week, he had very little time to think about anything but his uncle and soup. Finally, he saw an ad placed by a firm which wanted an assistant controller at $15,000 a year. Going against all our advice, he answered it by merely addressing the personnel manager who sponsored it. His counselor was furious.

"Why do you pay us a lot of money and then not listen to us?" the counselor asked. "Well, now it's done we will have to do something abut it. Your original letter will be lost with a lot of others, so write directly to the president."

He did, enclosing a résumé, of course. He wrote: "Although I am employed with my uncle making soup, I do not take much pleasure in swilling around this gooey liquid, and therefore I have decided to enter clearer waters. I am interested in your company because of the vast difference between your business and soup. I would like to chat with you and show you what I have to offer. I would like to call your office. . . ."

He had no chance to call the president. The president called him and, with a chuckle in his voice, said, "Young man, I'm delighted to find that there is at least one person in New England who is intelligent and knows how to make decisions."

In other words, he was telling Mr. X that he had not been fooled by the letter—he knew his personnel department was being bypassed.

"Come on in and see me."

A day or so later, Mr. X met the president, who was still chuckling. He went over Mr. X's résumé, smiled, and pushed a buzzer. In came the personnel manager. The president said, "I want to introduce Mr. X, who is a genius. Take him down to the controller." So, the personnel manager—with two hundred letters answering his ad still unopened—took Mr. X to the controller.

Now the controller was no fool. He knew the emotional man he worked for. So, well knowing where his bread and butter came from, he talked with Mr. X for a few minutes and hired him. I will skip some of the details, except to say that Mr. X was a worried lad when his first paycheck was delayed. He began to wonder whether he was working for a real company in a real world because of the weird way he was hired.

He need not have worried. After a few days, the ebullient president called him in. "Mr. X, I delayed your check because I have changed your salary from fifteen to eighteen thousand. It would be an insult to pay anyone of your intelligence fifteen thousand. And, by the way, you will be getting twenty in six months if you do as well as I expect you to do."

That is a gem—a true if unusual case. But the president in this case illustrated a tendency common to many executives. A boss will never forego an opportunity to demonstrate that his men cannot live without him.

Number 10: The Confetti Letter; the Turnover Letter

Letters are a tenth way to get a job. The confetti letter is a hard-sell letter sent to a hundred or more firms to call attention to your existence and to interest them in hiring you. It covers 3 to 5 percent of the market. A confetti letter campaign should be used only for long-distance relocation—it is a very poor approach to use when you are already in the area, able to make personal calls.

No résumé should be sent with a confetti letter for two reasons. First, the confetti letter is extracted from your résumé, so the pertinent facts are included. Second, if a résumé is included, your letter may not be read by an executive; it will be shunted directly to the personnel department by his secretary.

Confetti letters lose their power in proportion to distance. If you are in San Francisco and send a hundred letters to San Francisco firms, you may get three or four favorable replies. If you send a hundred from San Francisco to Los Angeles, you may get only two. If you send two hundred to New York, you will be lucky if you get one.

For the confetti letter, you go to your business library and look up all the firms you are interested in working for and write down the names of their presidents and the addresses of the firms. Group your lists geographically so that your letters can go out to New York, say, at the same time. The reason is this: If a New York firm is interested in you, it may offer to pay your transportation to New York for an interview. Other firms in New York may reply, "We would be very happy to chat with you the next time you are in this area." They are not going to pay transportation, but you will have additional prospects when you arrive in New York at some other firm's expense.

Each copy of the confetti letter should appear to be your own single original typescript. To achieve this illusion, they should be printed or lithographed—it is not expensive. They should be marked "Confidential." An effective confetti letter would read something like this:

Dear —————:

Although I am employed with the ABC Corporation as Manager of Research Planning, I am seeking the position of Director of New Product Development.

[or]

Subsequent to relinquishing my position with the ABC Corporation as Manager of Research Planning, I am seeking the position of Director of New Product Development.

My background includes over twenty years' experience in management of research and development, new product marketing, personnel selection, customer service, quality control, and product packaging and distribution.

Examples of my effectiveness are:

—Originated and managed a research project which developed a new patented inhibitor required for sales of isocyanates and blowing agents without patent license costs or litigation.

—Managed the preparation and negotiations of the first fluorocarbon food additive petition approved by the U.S. Food and Drug Administration. Negotiated contracts for sales of the product to national marketers.

—Developed test methods, as chairman of technical committees, which have become industry standards. Developed chemical product labeling and safe-handling requirements, and secured approval of regulatory officials.

I hold a PhD in Organic Chemistry and was teaching fellow, University of _____ , and a BS in Chemistry, University of _____ .

I would welcome the opportunity to talk to you or to a relevant executive in your firm. I am available for an interview at your convenience.

May I hear from you?

Sincerely,

[No résumé enclosed]

A confetti letter written for you by a top executive is twice as powerful as your own. An executive who knows you well might be happy to send out a confetti letter under his own name. In that case, construct one for him to sign, a letter very similar to your own:

Dear Mr. ——————:

I have learned in confidence that Mr. ——————, who is presently employed as Manager of Research Planning at the ABC Corporation, is seeking to make a career change. Prior to his present position, he had several years' experience with the —————— Corporation and —————— Company. I have known Mr. —————— for some ten years, personally and professionally, and I am impressed as much with his personal attributes as with his professional qualifications. Indeed, the level of his performance is unusual. He . . . [here a list of your clear achievements].

He is forty-five years old and is in good health. It occurred to me that a man of his caliber would be of interest to your organization, even though you might not have a current opening. I suggest it would be of interest to you to have a chat with Mr. ——————. Please feel free to contact him at —————— [your address] and to use my name.

> Sincerely yours,
> *Signed by an officer of*
> *a corporation; someone*
> *important*

Such a letter would have much greater power than your own because it is generally felt that anyone in a position of power will not stick his or her neck out for someone unless there is substantial confidence in that individual.

Do not expect immediate answers to your confetti letters. If they are to have any value at all, they must be sifted by the executives concerned — they must have an opinion of you before they can reply.

I started you off on a round of four hundred companies which could give you a job — if you hit at precisely the right time. I explained that it was a time equation, but I did not tell you how to solve the equation. I now have shown you ways to get a job in the published area of the market — where there is a known job. This can be done through newspapers, an employment agency, a consulting firm, or a recruiting firm. These methods cover only about 20 percent of your job market, but they solve the time equation. You go to an interview where a job is available. But the time equation has been solved for many other people beside yourself, so your chances of getting the job are limited.

We have talked of the confetti campaign, which is really like shining a light on the whole market at one time to reveal any jobs that may be available. A confetti campaign can solve the time equation. It is a quick burst which reveals the market in one bright, brief flash. If you are employed and feel no urgency about your job change, a better choice is the turnover letter. It solves the time equation with a time bomb to say, "I know you do not have a job for me now, but turnover may produce one and I'd like to register for it in advance." You may send out only one, two, or three of these at a time because you plan to follow them up by calling for an appointment. This type of letter makes a good substitute for personal phone calls to firms in your local area as well, if you are too busy to make the calls. Here is a sample:

Dear [*senior executive*]:

Although I am employed as ——————— at XYZ Corporation, I have decided, confidentially, to make a change. The accompanying notes illustrate my purposes and qualifications.

Now I do not expect, of course, that you would have such a position available at this time. I am, however, genuinely desirous of joining your firm. In the course of growth and change in your company, there will undoubtedly be positions I could fill to our mutual advantage.

I wish to acquaint you with what I have to offer so that I may be given consideration at the opportune time.

I will call your office within the next few days to arrange a brief appointment at your convenience.

Sincerely,

If you are sending the letter to a firm at some distance from your own area, you of course adapt it to the fact: "I expect to be in [Chicago, New York, Los Angeles] during the week of ——————. I will call your office on my arrival to arrange a brief appointment at your convenience."

We have covered ten ways to get a job—some of them not very good, some of them excellent. We have covered the *published* section of your market. Before we consider the *unpublished* market, by far the more promising and productive, let's take a little time to talk about some helpful techniques and procedures.

7 Getting Yourself Invited Back

There are certain techniques which can help you in your market campaign.

What should your attitude be? We will start out with a maxim: *You will go out into the market with obtainable objectives.* You want to be success-conditioned. You do not want to go into any room without coming out with what you had in mind. Success brings success.

If you should come into my office, I know very well I would sell you my services because I am convinced you should buy them and that I can sell them. I could not conceive of not selling you, because I am success-conditioned. But if I saw twenty people and none of them bought, I would be shuddering away from the next one who came in. The shoulder that quivers invites the lash. People will take you at the value you give yourself.

How can you be assured that you can always be success-oriented? By going out with a reasonable objective.

In the published section of the market, you have only one goal. Suppose a job is available and you are invited in for an interview. What is your objective? "Well," I can hear you say, "I was sent out by an employment agency, and I know the agency has sent others. My objective is the same as the other candidates: to get the job."

Well, excuse me, but your objective is stupid and ridiculous and inane.

No one at your level — referred by an employment agency or in answer to a newspaper ad — ever got a job on the first interview.

The mathematical chances of anyone hiring you on the basis of one interview are impossibly low — perhaps one in a thousand. So, if you go into an interview room pushing for a job, you are there under the wrong compulsion. Not only that, you hamper the interview by your "I-want-a-job" attitude.

The interviewer's job is to evaluate all candidates for a position. But you are consciously or unconsciously putting up a fight. Instead of allowing the interviewer to evaluate everyone tranquilly, you push with an antagonistic purpose.

Mr. Such-and-such put an ad in the newspaper. He needs a representative in Bangkok or somewhere. You are one of ten applicants, and he is not about to give any of you a job at the first interview even if you stand on your head at his command. First, he is going to take a good hard look at all ten of you. He is going to evaluate and think. Then he will reduce the number of applicants to three and invite these chosen three back. He may not offer the job until a third or even a fourth interview.

Under these conditions — which universally exist — what should your objective be? *The greatest objective you can have is to get the next interview.*

You can create the desire in the mind of the interviewer to invite you back for further evaluation in a smaller field of candidates. It is very simple. Listen to him. Help him evaluate your usefulness in terms of what he needs. Show enthusiasm. Point out what you can contribute. Act this way, and you will never have to ask for anything for yourself.

You adopt the attitude of an enthusiastic, attentive listener. The interviewer will do the talking. He will describe the job. He will ask some questions. When you are asked questions, you will imagine you are on the paying end of a long-distance call to Moscow — expensive — and you will be brief. The interviewer will ask most questions simply to assure himself that you are alive and will move quickly to the next phase of the interview. An intelligent look indicates you understand. That you understand means you are able.

You have to realize that when you are interviewed in the published area of the market, the interviewer is on your side at the start. Keep him there. Remember, he has a problem of his own — he has to fill a job with the best-qualified person he can find. It is to his interest that you be right for the job, for that would solve his problem. He will actually help you to be right for the job and stretch any reasonable point in your favor.

This fine situation is usually spoiled by your big mouth — talking too much, coming up with some statement which prevents the interviewer from reading something into your expression that he wants to see there.

Listen. Listen with an intent, intelligent look on your face. Ask any reasonable question which can help you and the interviewer to establish your validity for the job. Do not ask questions about salary, Blue Cross, vacations, your chances for promotion, or anything of that nature. Do not ask anything for yourself.

If there are ten candidates for a job, your chances are at least 30 percent to be invited back for a second interview. In actual fact, you make it a 95-percent chance by looking intelligent, keeping quiet, being brief, asking the minimum number of questions, and then sending a thank-you letter.

Your most effective move for getting the next interview — your highest objective — comes after you leave the room. Take some notes on your interview and immediately write a thank-you note to your interviewer. Immediately.

A thank-you letter is the most powerful weapon you can use — and it is a secret weapon. Very few people in any walk of life, in any part of the world, ever think to send one.

The thank-you letter is a second contact with the person you want to interest — the interviewer. To understand this, you must realize that there is no time in the realm of the emotions. If you and I were to work together for fifty hours and then part, we would not regard our relationship as particularly close—we might not even be well acquainted. But suppose you see me one hour every week for fifty weeks—we would both regard our relationship as very close. It is the same thing with a thank-you letter—your letter acts as a second encounter with the interviewer. It brings you into his mind again and, since you have written a thoughtful and appreciative letter, you are also in his emotions. And you can be almost certain that your letter will be the only thank-you he receives. In the whole of my career—and I handled many hirings—I can recall having received only two thank-you letters after an interview.

Here is how I see the human mind in this relation. Attached to the conscious mind is a box about four yards long and two yards wide and very deep. It is called the "self-validator box" and, although its actual physical presence has never been discovered, it is always present. Each of us has a little postal clerk whose duty it is to open the self-validator box every hour or so to see if there are any new deliveries. Are there any things which I can feel really pleased about? Have I been validated recently? The box, as I have shown is very large—we always anticipate a huge mail that does not, in fact, always come in.

Now your interviewer opens up his self-validator box one morning and finds a nice little letter from you. Dear Mr. Interviewer: I was really stimulated by yesterday's interview. Your reference to this or that, or your response to my question about this or that, made me look forward to the day I might join your organization. In passing, may I say that I have never been interviewed as pleasantly and efficiently in my life. . . ."

When your letter turns up, Mr. Interviewer has to be pleased. He has looked into his self-validator box and found self-validation. What a moment! He reads your compliments, probably more than once, and is almost forced to think, "This one *must* be intelligent." Then out of the crowd of faces he interviewed the day before, your face will stand out stark and clear. And he associates it with a very pleasant half hour he spent with you — a candidate who really made his job easy. The other candidates, he remembers, were a pushy lot.

To repeat: A thank-you note is the most powerful weapon you can use.

Now I will say something which seems almost incredible until you analyze the depth of your action. Here at my counseling firm we seldom have a client who does not get in at the kill even when he is not the most qualified candidate. This is because the client has left in the mind of the interviewer some good thoughts — as you can do: "She was thoughtful, bright, and pleasant. Now it's true that she doesn't have a degree in engineering and we need an engineer, but at the least we could bring her back for another look. Maybe there is something we can find for her. . . ." Our clients do not always get the job under these conditions — sometimes they are in competition with persons more highly qualified than they — but they almost invariably get down to the last interview.

Hiring is such a nonclinical thing. Everybody would like to make it scientific, but it all ends up very human. We cannot help ourselves. We *are* human.

Later on, we will discover many more aspects of interviews. But as a start, master this chapter so that the methods described become second nature to you. There is no mystery to any of them. All of them are simple — simple matters of courtesy and common sense. *And they work.*

8 The Referral Campaign – and Method Number Eleven

Now we introduce method Number 11 – the most important – the gentle art of getting the job you want without ever asking for one. We enter the unpublished section of the job market, which covers 80 percent of the jobs available to you. Let me repeat what I have said earlier: The most important thing to understand is that in the unpublished area – 80 percent of the job market – about half of the jobs available to you are potential jobs, not current jobs. They are jobs which might not even exist. But potential jobs can be created; three out of ten are. The created job is the prime job, because you build it with the person who is going to employ you. There is no competition. No salary or other conditions are preset. Everything is open to negotiation.

So your chief tool is the referral – a plan to allow you to be passed from one executive to another, always with a favorable reference, until you and your job meet.

In the published section of the job market, your highest objective was to get the next interview – to survive the winnowing out of candidates and be in on the kill when you were after a known job.

Your purpose in the unpublished section of the market changes drastically. It is no longer to get the next interview. *Your highest objective now is to make a deeply favorable impression on the people you call on* — presidents and vice presidents and department heads — those who can give you the job you really want. Realistically, you cannot always reach the top executives, nor should you. A reasonable goal would be to be referred to those who are two levels above your level or the level you wish to reach.

You do not ask them for a job. You make it clear that you would very much like to be considered for a job, but also that you are realistic enough to know that a job may not be available. You are there to ask advice of one who is experienced and successful.

Once you have made a favorable impression, your interviewer automatically will evaluate you for a job — if there is any relevancy between his world and yours, his needs and your capabilities. If you make a favorable impression and there is no relevancy between what you have to offer and his world, he will want to help you in any way he can. The way he can help, without peril to himself, is to refer you to other men on his level in business who might be able to help you with advice.

You want a job, but you ask for advice.

At the same time, you indicate that you would not refuse a job.

We had one client who entered an executive's office and, misreading his lines a bit, immediately declared, "I want it perfectly understood that I do not want a job here." He was perfectly understood and his interview lasted about three minutes. He had wasted the time of a busy executive and could only have left the impression that he was a fool, which is not the kind of impression to leave behind under any circumstances.

Why do I lay such stress on the referral interview? Because it puts you into the real world of economic problems, in an executive's office, where these problems bear the hardest. All there is in the mind of a senior executive is this real world of economic problems, hopes, and goals and, at the end of the road, a cash register.

He has an organization chart which is designed to help him solve these problems—but the chart is only the curve that fits the organization of today. He will be delighted to change the chart any time he can see a better way to organize his staff so the cash register will ring a more beautiful tune. We know that three out of every ten jobs never existed until those who hold them entered the picture. These jobs were created around the personalities of these people, created around their talents and the right mood in the room.

So, when you deal with senior executives, it is your talent, your personality, and the impression you make which are the elements that can suggest the solution of his given problem or set of problems. If a job is tailored for your talents and personality, you obviously have eliminated any competition.

Before we explore the workings of referrals further, let us consider one special aspect of their usefulness: their value to the man or woman who fears discrimination in the job market. If you are a member of a special group and think you may be vulnerable to this social evil, do not feel lonely. Grounds for discrimination are innumerable, and the situation is complicated by the fact that every group that is discriminated against, in its turn, discriminates against others. If you are black or white, Chinese, Indian, Puerto Rican, Spanish, Irish, or Italian, Communist, Birchite, Democrat, or Republican, a hawk or a dove, homosexual, lesbian, hermaphrodite, or sexless, fat or thin, short or tall, bald or hairy, one-legged or one-armed, very old or very young, blind, deaf, or mute, blue-, brown-, or hazel-eyed, squinting, stuttering, or muttering, Catholic, Jewish, Protestant, Muhammadan, Buddhist, or atheist, and are in fact alive, you are likely to be discriminated against by some group, somewhere, at some time.

What safeguards can a person take to avoid discrimination? The surest area is to use the referral method of getting a job, not to use letters, agencies, or advertisements. On the referral road of a job search, your interviewer, in recommending further people to speak to, will automatically refrain from giving you people who are likely to discriminate. It has been our personal experience that however a group is discriminated against in general, they have rarely been discriminated against when following the referral route. This is for a very human and natural reason. If you are, for instance, Jewish and you ask me for the names of other executives to talk to, and I think of some people and then recall that they do not ordinarily employ Jews, I will refrain from giving you their names. Instead I will search in my mind for the names of those persons who to the best of my knowledge do not discriminate against Jews. So if you are in one of the innumerable groups who risk discrimination, your safest road is the royal road to job search, that of the executive route through referral.

As I've already indicated, however, avoiding discrimination is only a side issue of the major argument in favor of taking this route. In itself the power of reaching an executive through a referral cannot be overemphasized. Let us suppose you are talking to a $100,000 a year executive. He does not turn off his brain while he talks. He never turns off his brain. It ticks along when he is talking to his wife, when he is working a crossword puzzle, when he plays with his children. It must be a fine machine, and it is a precision machine, because he is getting $100,000 a year for it, and it is now working on your problem. You have asked his advice and he has gone over your background and objectives. He may not have a position for you, but he is subjected to a variety of conditioning and mental processes instantaneously. When you ask him to suggest someone at his level for you to go to, he will not send you to a man who is firing half his staff. He will send you to another $100,000 executive.

Once again, you will be in the presence of another $100,000 mind looking at your problem. This is a refining and redefining process. After you have been through ten or fifteen such minds, you will have occupied some $1,000,000 worth of brainpower at no cost to yourself. This is surely infinitely better than fifty or sixty random interviews.

The only way to locate yourself properly is to prospect gently through the offices of relevant senior executives, quietly exposing what you have to offer until there is a matching of interests — and a job for you.

"Well and good," I hear you say. "It is easy enough to speak glibly about exposing yourself to senior executives. There is only one teensy little drawback—I don't know any senior executives."

Let's see. First of all, you may know one or a few executives, if you think long and hard enough. The task before you immediately is to draw up an "A" list—a list of people you have met in your life, however tenuously you know them, who are in a position to give you a job you want. You put them on the A list even if you hate their guts, even if you would never work for them and know they would never give you a job. What you are interested in is their power—they are in a position from which they dispense jobs. Geography is not important. If you know an executive in Hong Kong who might know an executive or several executives in the area you choose to work, that name goes on the list. You will need very few names on your A list, but the more names you can put down, the safer you will feel.

There is a second list to be made out, the "B" list. On the B list are people who could not possibly give you a job but who know people who could be on your A list.

Let me give you an example. We once had a client who knew a world-famous singer. That singer could not possibly employ our man, a controller. But the singer knew presidents of corporations and other executives by the dozens. The singer invited our client to his home one weekend. There he introduced him to important executives. That is the way our client's A list started.

Few of us know world-famous singers. But you may know an author with lines to A-list people. You may know an attorney whose friends or clients should be on your A list. Put her name on the B list and inquire about her connections, any connections which might help you to get a name on your A list. The A list is where you want to arrive at all times. You see a B in hope of being referred to an A.

You must construct a "C" list only if you find yourself marooned in the desert with no human resources at all—a very rare situation. Your C list is a list of people who live by people—a certified public accountant, your dentist, the minister of your church, professional associations, chambers of commerce, relatives. There are dozens of people you can put on the C list.

Time out for a sketch which nevertheless illuminates a truth. A man will say, "I don't know anybody. If I don't know anybody, how can I make up any kind of list?" So we ask him to think a bit.

"Well, I know a bartender who's pretty smart."

And we say, "All right. Start there."

So our man meets the bartender and says, "Mr. Bartender, you are a friend of mine and I need advice. I do not think you can give me the advice I need directly, but can you suggest a friend who might advise me?"

"Well," says the bartender, "I don't meet too many people in this joint. But I do know Harry, the barber, and he's a pretty smart guy."

So our man goes to Harry, the barber, and he says, "Harry, our mutual friend, the bartender, suggested I come to you. I need some advice. I don't think you're the man who can give it to me, but perhaps you might know someone who could."

Harry, the barber, thinks for a minute. "Some pretty smart guys come in here," he says. "Hey, I cut the governor's hair once in a while. I've known him a long time. I'll bet he'd give you some advice if I talked to him."

So, even though our man had to climb up from a low spot on the totem pole, he got to the top. I use this sketch to illustrate the fact that no one is so destitute that he or she cannot compile a list of proper contacts — the ones which produce interviews with the A list.

"The governor" is a prime example of a man on an A list. He very probably could not offer you a job which would interest you, but he certainly is in a position to give you advice and to refer you to another A-list person who could give you further advice and, possibly, the right job. The executive's field is not relevant: he or she can be in shipping, in museums, in advertising, in manufacturing, in hotels. The common denominator for the executives on your A list is the fact that they are individuals who can give advice, who can refer you to others of high standing or, quite possibly, give you a job in their own organization.

The lists, as I have shown, can begin anywhere. A friend down the street may be happy to show you he has powerful friends and give you some referrals. Many people forget their relatives — or, rather, stay away from relatives purposely. Relatives are important. Some of them may be in important positions, but we prefer to stay away from them. We say, "Oh, no! I'm not going to that old geezer. I ran away with his darling niece twenty years ago and he's never forgiven me." But what really happens if you write that terrible-tempered uncle a nice letter?

"Dear Uncle Scrooge: I have a problem, and because of your wisdom and experience I think you can help me. I need the advice of a man of discernment." Uncle Scrooge shows the letter to his wife, Aunt Molly, and says, "Well, that kid's finally come to his senses. Maybe I ought to see him." Possible? Possible.

Another route to an A list is through the alumni of your university and graduate school. "Dear Alumnus: You are a fellow graduate from good old Siwash and I have a problem. I do not expect you to solve my problem but I do know your experience can be helpful to me."

Could such a letter be detrimental to you? It is probable that many — maybe most — of your college alumni are more successful than you. They are presidents of corporations, presidents of colleges, senators, and congressmen. In general, anyone from your own college will see you. A Stanford graduate has an "in" with every other Stanford graduate, and the same goes for Harvard, Vassar, Cornell, and every other college in the land. And, of course, for fraternities and sororities.

There is another source of contacts: professional organizations to which you may or may not belong. Say you are in marketing. Perhaps a letter to the organization of marketing representatives in your area would produce a response from another person in marketing. He or she should be two levels above you, but is valid to go to for advice.

Editors of trade magazines and other publications are good contacts, whether you know them or not. It is their job to be acquainted with the executives in their field.

And, if you are employed, you can approach anyone of equal rank and they will see you because of a community of occupation. "Dear Broker: I am a productive though not very happy customer's representative in the Peanut Brokerage Corporation and I need advice from a fellow broker."

I have mentioned the minister of your church. Mention your problem to him; part of his calling is to listen to problems. He quite possibly has some very hefty members in his congregation and could say to you, "I'll be happy to talk to my employer about you. It will be a relief for both of us — the first time I haven't had to ask for money."

A little imagination can start you off toward the A list. You owe money to the Bank of Little Trust. "Dear Manager of the Branch Office," or "Dear Vice President: I am Mortgage No. 9763 and I pay more or less promptly every month. I have a problem and I believe a short talk with you could be helpful. I need to talk to someone of your business experience and acumen." The banker will answer, you owe money. He or she does not want you to have too many problems and will be flattered to be asked.

Members of your fraternal organizations can help. If you are a member of the Weasels or the Bears or the Elephants, you have a legitimate call on the sympathy and experience of your brothers. There are dozens—hundreds—of sources for contacts.

To cite all these ways of getting contacts is actually redundant. If you can come up with three or four names, you will have all you need. For, once you are referred to an executive on the A list, he or she will suggest other contacts to you, and the B and C lists, which may have been necessary when you were conducting a random search, are no longer necessary. You will be referred from one executive to another — referred by a person who has talked with you, seen what you have to offer, and on whom you have made a most favorable impression.

Now what I am going to say may seem odd to you: The first people to mark on your A list are your ex-employers, even if they once took you by the nape of the neck and threw you into the street. The less you want to see them, the more important it is for you to see them whether you are employed or out of a job. There are a number of good reasons for this.

The first reason is that you want a good reference. Former employers might give you a good reference automatically, but you want more than that. Perhaps they have not seen you for four or five years. If you go back, you revitalize their prior pleasant experiences with you, and when someone calls for a reference their voices are alive with a sense of renewed acquaintance. If you have moved from the area of prior employment, write a letter to rekindle a remembrance of your pleasant association. Or you might telephone your former employer on a Sunday when the rates are low.

Many of our clients got offers from former employers, even though they had been fired. That may seem curious, but it is really quite simple to understand: When they hired you originally, you impressed these people very much. You did a good job for them and then you were laid off, generally for reasons completely different from the ones you believed or the ones they told you. And, even had you been at fault, the minute they got rid of you, your values grew and your faults disappeared. For example, say you were fired because you were too lenient with your people. They replaced you with a twisted, tough guy who went around chopping heads off wherever he could. Two months after they fired you, they were sorry they let you go.

There are three reasons for going back to former employers. One is to reactivate their memory of you to ensure a good reference. The second is that ex-employers are a very good market for your talents because they bought you before and may be tempted to try you again. The third reason is to correct a bad impression and ensure a good reference.

I remember talking about this idea to a client who said, "I'll never go back to So-and-so. He hates my guts and I hate his."

"You didn't rob the till or do anything illegal, did you?"

"No, nothing like that," he said, "but I left under very adverse conditions. My boss threw me out."

"All right," I said. "Tell me about it."

"I was working for a slave driver," he said. "He made us

come to work at seven in the morning, an hour before anyone else, and he worked us an hour longer at night. Then, because he worked on Saturdays, he made us report, too. We got no extra pay for this because we were exempt from overtime.

"I worked his hours, all right, but I got madder and madder about it, and one day I slammed into his office and told him off. 'If you don't give me a hundred dollars more a month I'll tell you what you can do with your lousy job.' Actually, I told him exactly what he could do with his lousy job. And then, even the slow-grinding wheels of that company speeded up to a point that my papers were processed and I was out within three hours. And every time anyone calls that company, they give me a lousy reference. I'm damned if I'm going back."

The client had gotten a bit worked up just recalling the incident. I let him calm down a moment and then said, "That man, the boss who threw you out, is the first man you have to see."

"How can I see him? I tell you he hates my guts."

"Let me ask you a question," I said. "Would you ever do anything like that again—rush in to see a superior and act as you did?"

"No, of course not."

"Then you have learned a lesson, and you must be grateful to anyone who teaches you a lesson. Sit down and write to him. Write something like this: 'I am leaving my present position and am jelling my career plans. You are one person whose wisdom rendered me a great service. At a time in my life when I needed a lesson, you taught me the proper way to act. I have never forgotten, I can assure you, and I thank you for it. I would like a few minutes of your time to chat with you. I need the advice of a man like you.'"

Well, the former boss greeted my client like a long-lost son. They spent two hours together, and then the old curmudgeon said, "Look, if anybody calls here for a reference, make sure they get to me." And he gave our client eight referrals—executives for him to meet.

What other result could be expected? We are all human

beings. We forget and we forgive. Suppose you were that boss. Imagine the fingers of accusation which could point at you. "Maybe I was unfair with this guy. God knows I overworked everybody in those days; I didn't realize it then but I do now."

And never forget there are some very large companies in this country. In Boston, I had a client who was fired at $15,000 from one of them. We got him back into the same firm in another department two weeks after he was fired—at $18,000. Another man was fired from a $27,000 job and got another job at the same company at $29,500—with his separation pay still in his pocket. So if you want to work for XYZ and come to me and say, "I tried XYZ, but they wouldn't hire me," I simply will not believe you. If a building has one door and sixty windows, I will try all the windows if I cannot get in through the door.

One more case. We had a client who had been fired from his job. He came into the office, a very dejected man. "I've got a very big problem," he said. "If you cannot help me, please tell me so. My problem is this. I've been out of work for a year and a half and I can't get a job because of bad references—and the references are true."

"What's the story?"

"It was during the steel strike," he said. "I was materials director for our company, buying scrap steel. There was a lot of scrap around and we did very well while the strike was on, but when the strike ended I was on the wrong side of the fence.

"We had about a million dollars of junk steel around and couldn't sell it for love or money. The company lost two hundred and fifty thousand dollars and I got the gate. Now, whenever anyone calls for a reference, they get the message that I am a scatterbrain—a nice enough guy, but dangerous. And the hell of it is I can't deny it."

One quick fact leaped at me from this recital. This man was being used as a scapegoat. No materials manager buys a million dollars' worth of anything without some vice president finance or vice president manufacturing knowing all about it. It never happens. On a transaction of such magnitude twenty people are likely to be involved.

What about the man who fired you?" I asked.

"Oh, he's a tough, rough guy."

"Is he honest?"

"Yes, he's tough, but he's honest. He shouts and hollers and he's a very rude man, but I will say he's honest."

"Well, let's think of a way you can speak to him in his own language."

On my advice, the would-be client acted his role in a small drama we concocted. He burst into the room of the man who had fired him, the tough guy. He didn't even say, "Hello," just burst in and started talking.

"Look, George, I know you hate my guts and that's a feeling I reciprocate too. I hate your guts, too, but there is one thing about you—you are an honest man.

"I've got a wife and four kids. I've been out of work for a year and a half. I've got to earn a living. Now, here is my résumé, the way I've been presenting myself. Half of it concerns you. Now, will you read the damn thing and tell me if it's all right?"

So the tough boss sat and read the résumé, made some suggestions, and advised our man to forget the role he had played in the purchase of scrap steel. "There were a lot of others mixed up in that," he said. The session ended with lunch and cocktails, and the problem was licked.

We are all humans. Humans forgive and forget.

The less you feel like going back to somebody you once worked for, the more you have to go back.

Now let's look at the firms you must approach. There are three types of firms; expanding firms, those which are growing, driven either by economic conditions or the brilliance of their management; contracting firms, those which are cutting back for a variety of reasons; and monopolistic firms, AT&T, electric and gas utilities, and so on.

It is typical of the *expanding firm* that it is deliberately, consciously, competitively understaffed at all times. Says the executive of such a company—since he is human and thus terribly rapacious—"This is the time to squeeze every extra dollar out of the market, show a tremendous record of growth, watch the stock go up. Then, perhaps, I can unload my stock, which I've had for ten years, and walk away with a whopping profit." Or, "We want to earn an extra million dollars' profit this year and we aren't going to hire anybody so long as we can squeeze blood out of the present staff."

The proof of this attitude is simple: the average working week of a top American executive is fifty-five hours a week.

Now add to all the other pressures which crush an executive the ever-present pressure of turnover. Never forget the tremendous power of turnover. Families in the United States move every three years on the average. Most of these moves are made because the economic supporter of the house changes his or her job.

There is a constant demand for new employees because of the turnover in jobs. There is a constant pressure of turnover on the top executive, which can be relieved any time the conditions are favorable — any time the senior executive thinks you are the right type of person, he or she can hire you and take some of the pressure off. That is one reason why three out of ten jobs are created jobs.

How can you take advantage of the pressure on a senior executive and make an actual job for yourself with an expanding firm? Very simply: by displaying the beauty of what you have to offer in such a way that the harassed executive sees you as the right person for a job to be done.

The *contracting firm* is the easiest firm in the world to get a job with and often the best. In times of shrinking business, overhead cannot be reduced. Fixed costs are just that: fixed. So management hits the soft belly and begins to fire people. Management generally over-fires and creates a situation in which, because of the firing, it finds itself in need of more people than ever — people that it had before the firing started.

Why is this? Whenever management begins to fire its people, the human equation enters. The executive says, "I won't fire you because you're related to the big boss. And I won't fire that fellow over there because he did me a favor a week or so ago." Firing is not a science and is certainly less than an art when the human equation enters, as it always does.

When management hired the people it is now firing, it spent thousands of dollars to tailor each individual to a particular job. Now the executive has to reshuffle what is left of the staff over a wider front, and shuffles everybody out of the right job and into a wrong one. The executive has thrown away a million dollars' worth of people — it now takes ten people to do the work nine used to do.

Furthermore, I, as the executive, miscalculated the demoralization which now floats over the friends of the missing. The best people, the ones I wanted to lose least, were the ones able to move the fastest and they did. And I forgot something else: turnover was eating up 18 percent of my people every year, and now the news is getting around that we are firing and the word is, "Don't go to work for XYZ. They're letting everybody go." So the normal, natural trickle of people which used to show up looking for work ceases, and I am now short of the people I have fired, plus the 18 percent I normally lost by turnover. I have created a need for more people by deliberately planning disorganization.

Under these circumstances — which are not exaggerated — is there any doubt that pressures are very great on the executive to hire a qualified person? You come along, well prepared, and meet the president of this struggling company and you say, "I really would like to work for you. I've got confidence in your company."

Do you think it would be difficult to create a position there? The poor executive, that rejected soul who feels hated by the whole organization, simply cannot refuse anyone who says sincerely, "I like you."

As for the *monopolies*, they are able to forecast their needs with great precision. So can you. You drop a time-bomb letter: "I have examined your program, and it seems you will have sixteen jobs of the type I am looking for within the next year — or ten years. I am applying now for the next position which becomes available. I have enclosed some notes which will show my qualifications. . . ."

You will already notice what I am doing: I'm making a sale to you. I am giving you these inner truths because they will work effectively for you. I am telling you that, by making conditions right, which is within your power, you can create a job for yourself in a firm you want to work for.

9 Interview Strategy

Armed with all this information, you can now begin your market campaign. You seek to be interviewed by people who can give you advice, possibly a job, and at the least, two referrals to other executives.

A word of caution here. Do not overschedule yourself. Schedule only one interview a day—preferably in the morning.

Now you check your A list, pick a name, and write something like this:

Dear ————:

Having recently relinquished my position, I am jelling my career plans.

[or]

Although I am employed, I have confidentially decided to make a change.

The accompanying notes will give you a picture of my purposes and qualifications.

While I would be delighted at the prospect of joining your firm, there, of course, may be no suitable opening at this time. [Or other suitable sentence depending on occupation of, or relationship with recipient.]

Nonetheléss, I feel that your advice would be helpful to me.

I will call your office to request an appointment for a few minutes of your time, at your convenience.

Sincerely,

Résumé enclosed.

When you are referred by one executive to another, you should write a letter along these lines:

Dear ———:

In the course of a conversation, ———, Vice President of the XYZ Corporation, suggested that your advice at this time would be of help to me.

Having recently relinquished my position, I am jelling my career plans.

[or]

Although I am employed I have confidentially decided to make a change.

The accompanying notes will give you a picture of my purposes and qualifications.

While I would be delighted at the prospect of joining your firm, there of course may be no suitable opening at this time. [Or other suitable sentence.]

With this in mind, I would very much appreciate an opportunity to talk with you. I will call your office to request an appointment for a few moments at your convenience.

Sincerely,

Résumé enclosed.

Question: *Can't the purpose of this letter be accomplished by telephone?*

Answer: *No, because you are going to call later to set an appointment. Depending on the degree of intimacy you have with the person you are asking to see, you might make the letter a* *little less formal: "(First name), I'm mailing you some background notes about myself. I need your advice and I think it would be very helpful to me if you have time to digest my problem before I see you. I'll call you later to see when there is a convenient time for us to talk."*

You must follow up such letters with a telephone call within forty-eight hours. If you wait more than forty-eight hours, your letter will be likely to trickle down to the last place you want it to reach—the personnel department.

Make your phone call with self-assurance. If you are employed, it pays to give your title. "This is Ann Bennet, the division controller at XYZ Corporation. Will you put me through to So-and-so; my call is expected." It's true — you said you would call.

If the secretary replies that your letter has gone down to personnel, you must say, "There has been a misunderstanding. I am not applying for a position. I would like to clear this up with So-and-so. Would you connect us, please?"

When the executive picks up the telephone, you say, "Of course I would like to be evaluated for a position, but it would be wrong of me to suppose you had one. However, I would like very much to chat with you for five or ten minutes. When may I come in?"

In some instances, you will run into people who refuse to see you — perhaps one in ten. In any event, ask who would be the proper executive in the firm to call on. The main thing is the tone of voice you use — a voice that is self-assured, relaxed, and courteous.

Question: *Is it more effective to have your secretary put the call through for you?*

Answer: *Oh, you are crafty. Of course it is better to have a secretary put in the call, and you know it very well. Here is the way it works. Your secretary calls up and asks for you to be put through to So-and-so. The receptionist says, "May I ask in what connection?" Answer, "It's personal." Magic word! You get put right through.*

Here is another word of advice. You can often get to top executives directly if you call very early in the morning. Many a corporation president gets to his office an hour or so before his secretary. He will answer the telephone if he knows his secretary has not arrived.

You get an appointment. Prepare yourself—find out a little about the executive's company. Find out the general objectives of the company, if you can. If not, you should at least know what the company does or what it makes.

Then, because you have been thinking about yourself, analyzing yourself, you already will have mastered certain truths. You know who you are and you know you are qualified for the job you seek. You have a proper image of yourself on paper. And, most important, you have the proper frame of mind. The key is always to be positive and constructive.

People mirror emotions. Attitudes are reciprocated. Positive feelings are returned for positive feelings; negative feelings are returned for negative. Enthusiasm is infectious. Condition yourself to be enthusiastic.

The day of the appointment arrives. You sit in the reception room of the executive's office. Mentally, you recite the purpose of your visit: My first purpose is to make a deeply favorable impression.

How do you create this favorable impression? By the courtesy of your approach and the warmth of your whole aspect. You can condition a man to be well-disposed toward you by making a genuine comment: "I certainly do appreciate your taking time out to talk with me, Mr. So-and-so. I know how busy you are."

When he asks you what he can do for you, ask if he has read your résumé. If he says he has not, hand him a copy and ask him to read it. This takes very little time.

If he says he thinks the résumé is good, say, "I am very pleased you like it. Which parts did you particularly like?" You want him to talk.

If he says he thinks it is a pile of junk, look disappointed and ask, "What was the part you didn't like?" Get him to criticize your résumé. You want him to talk.

You must be prepared for his answer by remembering what your résumé does. It states clearly what you want; it logically relates what you want to elements in your background; it shows you in your finest clothes within the truth; it is brief enough to provoke questions; it reflects your education and the kind of person you are. If your résumé accomplishes those five things, it is right.

With this in mind, listen carefully when your interviewer criticizes it. Whatever his criticisms, make careful note of them on the spot but if they do not relate to the five things your résumé is designed to do, do not be disturbed. If they will not enhance the clarity of your purposes or the logic you have used to relate your background to those purposes, if they will not help your résumé to show your finest qualities more effectively, or help it to provoke questions you want to be asked, the critic's suggestions are valid but they apply to a different animal from the one you are talking about. So write them down, thank him sincerely, and throw them in the first trash can you see. If his criticisms seem valid for you, refine your résumé after careful thought.

What really happens when a man says, "I think this is a lousy presentation"? In many cases, he is saying, "Gosh, man, you're terrific, but you've done a horrible job of presenting yourself." If you scarcely know each other, how did he happen to find that out? By the very instrument he is damning. "I think this is lousy" really means "I think you are better than the presentation." But how did he find out? By the résumé; it seems to have done its job very well. Your question "How do you think it could be improved?" may actually produce only a minor, and possibly helpful, criticism.

And usually your interviewer wants to be helpful. Cast your mind back a bit and ask, "Why did he allow me to come to see him?" There are only two reasons a person will see you — out of courtesy, or because there is a job for you. If the interviewer has a job and wants you, he will read more into your assets than you yourself ever will. If he sees you out of courtesy, he will not want to hurt you.

Frequently, he opens with a standard question: "Tell me

about yourself." You want to hear that question because it means "Make me a sale."

Your answer is intelligent. You know your major talents and you ask, "Would you like to hear about my management experience or my market development or my work in personnel?" If he chooses an area, it is most likely the area of his own interest. Then you give a brief outline of your experience in the area he has selected. Pick up two or three achievements and speak of each briefly. Then you can ask the logical question. "That illustrates my marketing competency. Is that the kind of marketing you have?"

Or he may say, "I don't care where you start. Start where you want to."

So the choice is yours. "Perhaps I'd better start with my management ability and experience. Let me refer to the time I was called on to reorganize the Philadelphia activities of the XYZ Corporation. I should tell you a little about the conditions which prevailed and what we had to do about them."

You talk a little bit about that, but if you don't see any great interest, skip to your next talent and achievement and sketch in the details. By being brief and listing your talents, you will readily see when an interviewer is interested. He has to relate to you somewhere along the line. If he has no problems in marketing, in people, in administration, or communications, or manufacturing, forget him. He's dead. Somewhere along the line, you will get responses; he will begin to talk. He may talk a great deal. We know the story about the president who talked steadily for two hours and was so struck by what a wonderful conversationalist an applicant was that he gave him a job.

When your executive is talking, never take the stage away. A good interview, in fact, is one in which the other person talks for two hours and you talk for ten minutes.

I cannot overemphasize the importance of responsive, intelligent listening. You must listen with a supreme degree of intelligence radiating from your eyes. Never pass over something you do not understand because, in that brief second, you will look stupid. If you do not understand what is being said, quickly interpose, "I didn't quite catch that. Could you explain?" Then, when the matter is explained, a look of enlightenment will appear on your face.

A word unsaid never has to be corrected. Physiologically, you have two ears and one mouth, which might suggest something to you. You must harken to Nature and resolve: "I will listen twice as much as I talk." It might even be better as, "I will listen ten times as much as I talk."

Let me illustrate. Suppose your interviewer says, "Tell me about yourself," and you start telling him the whole wonderful, beautiful life story of you. As you ramble, the interviewer has to do all the work: "That bit about school doesn't mean anything — we've all been to school. That job he did in Vietnam was interesting — I'll have to remember that. . . ." He has to wade through, sort out, categorize, and edit your remarks.

Here is a concrete example. My car has been in an accident, so I go to a dealer.

"My car is smashed," I say.

The man is very pleasant. "I'll get help for you," and he calls over the spare-parts expert, Fritz Urzog. Urzog is also very pleasant. He leads me to the parts room. "Here are all the parts we have," he says. "There are fifty-seven hundred of them. Just pick out the ones you need."

I may scratch around through the spare parts for a half hour or so before I realize how ridiculous I am and leave. I go to the next dealer and tell him about my car trouble.

"No problem," he says, and he calls Urzog II.

Urzog II looks at my car, gets out a piece of paper and a catalog, and makes a list. "Left fender, Part No. 7659, price unassembled, $54; labor estimate, $18.20. . . ." He goes down the list, and at the end he tells me what parts are needed and what the job will cost. Whom do I do business with?

How unreasonable you are if you go into an executive's room and tell your whole bloody inventory of parts and make him or her work to sort out the likeable ones. Instead, you can help by offering the choice of the parts of your inventory that are of interest and give brief and to-the-point answers.

We are all used to the hard sell, yet we all forget the greatest merchandising method on earth is silence. Think of the enormous sum of money invested across the nation and around the world in thousands of storefronts that silently display merchandise and give you the positive role of going into the shop and making a purchase from a living salesman — who, quite possibly, will talk too much.

In an interview, there is a time for muteness and a time for speech. The time to talk is when you are being questioned in an area of your expertise. In such a situation you can talk to some degree; you know what you are talking about, and your speech does not raise problems for the other person. Make your speech solve problems. Make it concise and to the point.

I am going to bring this first interview to a close as rapidly as possible and then go on to special situations which you may face.

Your executive has read your résumé and has commented on it. You have answered questions and it is clearly time to go. Pleasantly and in your own way, rise and thank the executive for the courtesy of being seen. "I really appreciate all that you have been able to suggest to me today. I can see my need to talk to others on your level. Not, of course, to ask them for a job, but to continue to broaden my market horizons — just to chat with them as I have with you. Could you suggest one or two people whom I might be able to meet and talk to for a few minutes?"

If you have made a good impression, your interviewer is almost certain to suggest other executives you might meet. But say he or she draws a blank — cannot think of a single name for you. In that case, would it not be intelligent to have prepared a list — the names of ten companies you would really like to work for and the names of their presidents? If your interviewer draws a blank, draw out your list.

"These are corporations I'd really like to work for — the kind of companies I think I would fit into. What do you think of them?"

Your interviewer will read the list. As he does so, he will comment. He will probably say three or four are fine companies. He might damn a competitor or two.

On the basis of his comment, you can then say, "Fine. I think it would be a good idea if I talked with ZYX Corporation. Do you know Mr. Such-and-such, the president there?" If your man says yes, you have a referral. You can then write to the president whose name was mentioned and say, "In a conversation with Mr. So-and-so, the president of ABC Company, he suggested that it might be a very good idea that I talk to you. . . ."

If he says he knows none of the presidents of the companies he recommended, you then ask, "Do you know any substantial people at JKL Company I could chat with?" and you might get a few names. But if your executive simply says, "I think it would be a good idea to talk to those people at JKL," go no further. Without lying, you have all you need—owing to the vanity of human nature.

Just look at your next tactic. You write to the president of JKL Company and say, "In conversation with Mr. So-and-so, he endorsed my idea that a conversation with you might be helpful at this stage of my career."

But, you say, Mr. So-and-so never suggested such a thing."

That is true, but the president of the JKL Company will read your letter in the manner best calculated to suit his vanity. The power of Mr. So-and-so's name will carry the day. And you have not lied. You do not say that Mr. So-and-so suggested you consult the president of JKL. You do say that Mr. So-and-so endorsed your idea that a conversation with the head of JKL might be helpful. The fact is he takes that as a compliment and a direct referral.

You say your thank-you and good-bye and your interview is over. You have made a good impression; you have a referral, preferably two or more. The interview was a success.

But perhaps you feel it was not a success. A word of caution is necessary here. Perfection is not necessary. There is room in human affairs for quite a few errors without any of them being fatal or even critical. Do not blame yourself for not performing perfectly. You will never perform perfectly.

And, if you performed below your standard of perfection,

you can correct whatever mistakes you made in a simple and logical way. I speak, once again, of the thank-you letter.

Let us review the nature and purpose of a thank-you letter. Our feelings and knowledge of other persons depend on the number of times we adjust the bands linking us to one another. The number of meetings, not the length of meetings, is the key. In the emotional area there are no clocks. You send me a letter and a résumé: we have met. You call on me for an interview: we have met again. Since you made a good impression, I have given you leads to other persons who might be helpful. By the standards we have set, you have had a successful interview.

Now you want to multiply the good impression you have made on me: you write me a thank-you letter *to turn me into a salesman on your behalf.*

Everyone you meet in your market campaign must receive a thank-you letter. Even if someone barked at you, you must thank him for his bark. There is always something genuine to thank someone for.

Your thank-you must be genuine and it must be just as flattering as it can be within the limits of your personality. I could say, "I love you," because I have a bubbly personality. You, perhaps, could not go so far. But you can go further than you might think, and I suggest that your thank-you letter be at the limit of your range. You cannot overflatter a person in an area of his genuine competence. If I see a good-looking girl, I might say, "You're the cutest little thing in Los Angeles." Anyone hearing my remark might think I was making the wildest overstatement. To the girl it would be, of course, an understatement.

Your thank-you letter—your extra dividend meeting—also gives you a chance to correct any statement you may have made that you are uneasy about. You can fill in some things you feel should have been covered in the interview—to make it more nearly perfect in your view.

And when you do find your new job, do not forget the people who helped you. Another little note to each is in order. "Dear So-and-so: I recall with pleasure our meeting on such-and-such a date. Were it not for the friendly advice you gave me I would not have succeeded as rapidly as I did in my search for a new position. You will be glad to hear that I am now controller at the ZYX Corporation. I want you to know that I will always feel indebted for your help." Such a letter should go to all those who listened to your problems and gave advice. As an added fillip, put these names on your Christmas card list every year. They will be happy to receive your greetings.

Now what have you accomplished? You have placed your résumé before an important executive. You have met him and made a favorable impression. By the interview, you have turned an important executive into a favorable center of information about your ability and availability. By your thank-you letter, a warm letter full of praise and thanks for the help the executive gave you, you have turned him into an active salesman for you. Obviously, the more executives you see — one, six, eight, sixteen — the stronger your sales force becomes. And in actual fact, you are bound to increase your armament in proportion to the acuteness of your problem. With the number of salesmen on your behalf increasing with each interview, your array of artillery finally becomes so great that your problem has to crack, and it does — it cracks in a number of ways: someone calls you for another interview; someone calls who has heard of a position he knows would fit you; someone calls who has a job.

You have been efficient. You have turned important executives into favorable centers of information about yourself and your problem, you have gotten leads to other executives, and, by your thank-you letters, you have recruited a staff of high-level, high-powered salesmen.

Question: *You make it sound very easy. What if it doesn't work so smoothly? I know I'm going to be depressed.*

Answer: *You can only be depressed when you are out of action. When you feel depressed, do something. It does not matter what action you take. Even if you do the wrong thing, you will recognize it and get back on the right track. Consider this* *happy thought: The world owes you a living. You are part of the world and have as much right as anyone to live — as long as your attitudes are positive.*

I repeat: Enthusiasm is infectious.
Condition yourself to be enthusiastic.
It can be done, and it is very important.

10 How to Move When the Interview's Lights Turn Green

As a general rule, the person who interviews you should do all or most of the talking. I have made that statement many times, and it is almost always questioned. "Suppose I get one of those people who just sit there and don't say a thing?" The answer, of course, is simplicity itself: the world's record for anyone keeping his mouth shut in the presence of another human being is thirty-one seconds. If you can keep your mouth shut for up to thirty seconds — it is very difficult — the other person will begin to talk.

Usually, he will ask the question "What are you looking for?" You tell him the kind of position you want, very briefly. He will then do all the exploration.

This can be very pleasant and stimulating — listening to an intelligent person explore your career. Dignified and enthusiastic listening — not obsequious listening — is profitable. As you are spoken to and questioned, you will see certain signs of interest, certain indicators of the interviewer's feelings. Since your objective is to create a favorable impression, be prepared to recognize these signs of interest.

There are seven green lights that can tell you the impression you are making and guide your actions. I say seven, although there may be seven million green lights—depending on the individual, the company, and the circumstances of the day. But there are seven sure green lights that recur all the time, regardless of circumstances. They are the ones you should look for.

The first green light may appear at the very beginning of your meeting. Your executive gets up to meet you, is extremely courteous, and seems to know all about you. When you are seated, he will reveal that he knows your résumé by heart, he knows your background, and he begins to talk easily about you. You can be sure that man is interested in you—for himself.

The other six green lights can appear—burning brightly—at any time during the interview.

The second green light is revealed by the way your man questions you. If he questions you intensely and makes careful note of your answers, he is interested in you. The questions are for himself and not to advise you.

A third green light blinks on if your man discusses his own problems endlessly. He is paying you a compliment by discussing his problems with you. Secondly, he very probably is wondering if you are the doctor—whether you can cure the ills he has.

Question: *Might not an executive who brings up his own problems be just picking your brains without any intention of hiring you?*

Answer: *Let us take your premise—that he brings up his problems even though he has no intention of hiring you. What do you do? You listen with restrained enthusiasm, relate his problems to your experience, and give him all the information you can. When a man is robbing you of your ideas, he is really preparing himself for the sudden need to hire you.*

A fourth green light shines when your executive introduces you to other executives of his company or suggests that you talk to other executives. By his action, he is referring you down, and to be referred down is tantamount to an instruction to hire.

Let me give you a horrible example of this. I was working for a company whose president sent me a real idiot one day—I was personnel manager and a lot of other things all wrapped up in one. I talked to this idiot for about ten minutes, figured he was no good, and did not give him a job. I could not live it down for six months. Every time I was in a meeting with the president, he made a point of saying, "Why don't you discuss that with Djeddah? He's the expert on people around here." I learned my little lesson. The next time the president sent me an idiot, I hired him like a shot and gave him $10 a week over our standard rate.

What the president meant when he sent these men to me was, "I don't know very much about these fellows but, as you are aware, I am a genius and I was impressed when I saw them. They will solve our problems." For me to shoo them away was to tell the boss that he was wrong, and we all know very well that the boss is never wrong except by his own consent.

A fifth green light, and this is very common, comes on when your executive begins to sell you his corporation. "We started in 1964 with a one-room shop and now we've got four factories. We've got a staff psychiatrist, and now we're thinking about giving our people cemetery plots. . . ." That is a bright and shining green light because he is trying to soften you up for a job with his sterling company by telling you about the marvelous world he lives in.

Another green light appears when your executive talks about a position unlike the one you are interested in. Your résumé indicated you want a controller's job. The executive thinks, "We already have a controller, a good man, and we certainly aren't going to fire him. But we do need a traveling senior auditor." So, although he knows you want to be a controller, he starts talking about senior traveling auditors. He is telling you, indirectly, that he is impressed by you and your talents—would you be interested in this other job?

Here a word about line versus staff jobs. It is very difficult for an outsider to step into a line job—a position which gives you direct responsibility for a firm's major effort, vice president marketing, vice president manufacturing, and so on. So if you have the capability for a line position, it would be well for you to make it clear that you are also interested in a staff job. Accepting a staff job allows you to be on the inside, to be accepted, and then develop plans which could lead to a line position.

As an example: as a staff employee, you might discover your company was not getting its share of government contracts. By developing a plan for capturing this market, it is very possible you would be put in charge of the execution of your plan and that ultimately you would achieve a line position as the person in charge of government sales.

It can be stated positively that line people look with extreme disfavor on an outsider who comes in to fill a line position.

The seventh green light comes on when your interview runs for more than thirty minutes. Thirty minutes is a long time for someone to interview you if he or she is not interested in you or does not have a job in mind for you.

Now, whenever one of those green lights turns on, you change the objective of the interview. No longer do you want to make a good impression and to get referrals; your new objective immediately becomes the next interview with this executive who is so interested in you.

Each individual will react to the green lights in his own way, but several ways suggest themselves. In the most heated part of the executive's talk—and when the conversation has run a proper time—you could stand up and say, "Mr. So-and-so, I've found this conversation fascinating, but I promised to take only a few minutes of your time. I'd really like to continue this discussion. May I come back next week?"

What does your executive say? One of several things. He may say, "Well, I *am* tied up today, but why don't you come in Tuesday morning at ten? We've got a lot more to talk about." Or, "Look, I've got time to go on now. Stay for a few more minutes." Or he picks up his phone and says, "Hold the calls, will you please, and don't let anyone disturb us for the next half hour."

He might say, "Well, I don't think we really have anything more to go through." At that point—when the strong want to weep—you return to your earlier objective: to get referrals to other executives.

I strongly suggest you smile rather than weep, smile grate-fully, and say something like this: "Mr. So-and-so, you've ob-viously been evaluating me and that is very flattering. What you have said encourages me in my purposes. You know I am trying to get maximum exposure to executives at your level. I want to ap-proach other people just as I approached you. I would be delighted to be considered for a job, but that is not my first purpose. My chief purpose is to benefit from their advice —just as I have benefited from yours. Could you suggest people whom I could see?"

Your executive has evaluated you; he has been impressed but he has no place for you in his organization. In most cases, he would be happy to suggest friends for you to talk to. He will prob-ably do some sifting for you. He will not send you to irrelevant people and let you waste their time. In his concern for his friends he is going to send you to relevant people and thus guarantee automatically that you won't waste *your* time.

If the executive cannot think of anyone at all, pull out your list of ten companies you would like to work for, get reactions, and you will get your referral. If the executive is of any standing, he will know people at those companies. He will probably feel quite relieved by the help your list gives him.

About one person in ten will not see you. Do not be upset by this. Don't waste time on the ugly customer. Don't hound him to death. There are nine others of equal standing who will be happy to see you. If your referrals come from the right person, anyone in town will see you.

To repeat: when you see the green lights come on, re-target for a further interview. You will probably succeed.

I want to emphasize as strongly as I can that this is the proper and only way to conduct an interview. If you want to forget every-thing I have told you, if you decide not to waste time and to go directly after a job, you will fail because you will not get any referrals from anyone. See what happens:

You come into Mr. So-and-so's office and you say, "Mr. Such-and-such suggested that I come to see you for a job."

What is Mr. So-and-so's reaction? His reaction will be, "Well, damn Such-and-such. Does he think I'm running an employment agency? And he didn't even have the decency to call me. I don't have any job and to hell with Mr. Such-and-such."

But if, following instructions, you go to Mr. So-and-so's office and say, courteously and in a dignified manner, "Mr. Such-and-such in a conversation with me the other day said he thought you were an executive who has the kind of experience which could be helpful to me at this time of my career. Neither Mr. Such-and-such nor I thought that you would have an appropriate position, although I would be delighted if you did, but he did think your insights could be very helpful to me."

Now what are Mr. So-and-so's reactions? "Gee, I haven't seen Such-and-such for months. A fine man. Thinks I have valuable insights. That's good to know."

In the instance when you directly sought a job, you may have hurt the relationship between two friends. In the indirect approach I suggest, you very probably have strengthened their relationship, reminding one fine man of the existence of another. And you have flattered Mr. So-and-so in the most powerful way. There is no compliment as powerful as the indirect compliment, just as there is no insult as powerful as the indirect insult.

Let me give you an example: if I come up to you and say, "Williams, you're a bloody fool," that is an insult. You will be infuriated. You will say, "Djeddah, come outside, I'll take care of you." Or you might argue it out, but the insult has been made directly and you can find ways to cope with it. But now suppose your secretary comes in one day and says, "I hate to say this, but Eli Djeddah said you're the bloodiest fool in San Francisco." That is much more infuriating than the direct insult because you cannot get back to me with it. You may accuse me of saying such a dreadful thing and I can deny it. You can think I'm lying, but there is nothing you can do about it.

Let's remember the girl I referred to as "the cutest little thing in Los Angeles." If I call her that directly to her pretty face, her immediate reaction is to hear the bells of caution ring. "What does this guy want?" she thinks. "Is he trying to get into bed with me or something?" If, on the other hand, she is talking to a girl friend who says, "What's with Djeddah? He says you're the most beautiful girl in Los Angeles," there are no price tags attached and the compliment has to be true. She knows it is sincere and her thoughts turn to me.

Burn this into your brain because it is genuine.

We have just come through a pleasant interview with green lights blazing all over the place. But it so happens that the green lights can be burning brightly and, all of a sudden, they all go out. This happens. And it is not because an executive has suddenly discovered you are an idiot, or detects alcohol on your breath, or that you suddenly look like a crook.

In nine out of ten cases, when the green light flicks out, your interviewer has suddenly thought of some reason — money or otherwise — why you cannot be hired.

Imagine this: You have taken the pains to prepare a résumé which will help you get a job at a level several thousand dollars above what you formerly earned and you have supported your desires — although no figure is stated — with a list of accomplishments. Now the interview proceeds merrily, green lights ablaze, and your interviewer suddenly thinks back to your résumé, and thinks, "This woman has to be worth twenty-five thousand, and we've never been in a position to hire that kind of talent." She might have a job at $17,000 but thinks, "To offer her seventeen would be an insult," so she says nothing. She will be very polite about it, but will not make you an offer. The green lights are dead.

But you are not defeated. At the very end of the interview, you say, "Ms. Johnson, I've got to ask you an important question. Based on my background, how much do you think I should be looking for?"

Your interviewer will then, in all probability, say, "Well, I don't know — but based on the background you've offered, I'd say twenty-five thousand."

You then smile a happy smile and say, "Ms. Johnson, that is exactly what I think I'm worth, but I don't expect to start at that."

The next question is almost inevitable. "How much did you expect to start?"

And your answer, "That would depend on the company, the kind of job, and future prospects. I can be quite flexible, and with the right kind of company I'm sure I would be reasonable. If I went to work for your company, I could be very reasonable, because from what I've learned here today this is a company I would like to work for."

The green lights might very well flash on again at this point. Ms. Johnson could very well be moved to say, "Sit down and let's talk some more."

Many people, not often exposed to a carefully prepared résumé, sometimes can read your salary five or ten thousand above your level. When that mistake occurs, corrective tactics are in order. A closed door can be reopened.

And even if nothing happens, it will not do you any harm to hear a top executive say she thinks you are worth $25,000.

11 Positive Answers to Tough Questions

Let us deal with some basic questions pertaining to your job campaign. Some of them come up in interviews. Others are in your head before you begin.

What about age?

In the late 1950s it was a problem for a man or a woman over forty-five to get a job. Earlier in that decade it was a problem for a man or a woman over forty to get a job.

The problem of the person over forty disappeared when the new generation began to attend graduate schools or had to complete military duty. The newcomers entered the job market later, and so age forty no longer was a barrier to seeking a job.

The problem for those forty-five and over was simply that they could not get jobs in the published section of the market. Since the published area is only approximately 20 percent of the whole market, their plight was not hopeless. But it meant that instead of going out on twenty interviews they had to go out on thirty before they found a firm or an executive who would not discriminate against them because of their age. That meant it was

50 percent harder for them to find a position but, on the basis of one interview a day, it meant thirty days rather than twenty—in absolute terms only ten days' more effort than their juniors'.

These older clients were helped by a fact of history called the Great Depression. The United States then had a population of 120 million and a very large number of them were out of work. So a curious but logical thing happened: people stopped having babies. The poverty of the 1930s was more potent than the Pill of the 1960s, and the result is that thirty-five-, thirty-six-, thirty-seven-, and thirty-eight-year-olds, the age group of upper-middle management, almost do not exist. So an employing firm has only two choices — take a risk and hire a very young person or get hold of someone who is forty-five or fifty. That situation will last, by all estimates, until sometime around 1980.

A person's age becomes an employment problem when he passes fifty-five. People are very reluctant to hire a person who is fifty-eight or fifty-nine. But, once again, it depends on the individual. If a man of fifty-eight goes in to be interviewed and looks physically fit and mentally alert, he may not have a problem; if he goes limping in, puffing from his long journey up a short flight of stairs, he will not be hired. It is a well-known fact that none of us really know how old we are until the day we die —a fact which will be revealed only at the ultimate minute.

What about education?

There is no question but that a man or woman with only a high school education is at a disadvantage in the executive job market. But if you can show supplemental education —night school or correspondence sources and a good work-experience record —your chances improve. Most people seeking executive positions can read and write, and that is enough of a rarity to set them apart.

How does a recession or depression affect your job campaign?

Depressed market conditions will impose some obvious differences on an intelligent approach to job search. This is because (a) there are fewer jobs in the agencies and a multiplication of applicants for them and (b) there are fewer jobs offered in the newspaper and again a multiplication of applicants; since the confetti letter refers to the same markets as the above categories, its effectiveness diminishes drastically in hard times. Getting a job is always the result of being interviewed by the right people. Now the job searcher has no control whatsoever over the generation of interviews in the above three areas. He registers with agencies, he answers ads, he mails out confetti letters, and then is reduced to a condition of hopeful impotence, waiting for invitations that in hard times are few and far between. On the other hand, the executive referral route, properly handled, is under the control of the job searcher. He can proliferate his interviews and increase his speed of exposure to compensate for the slackness of the economy. In times when unemployment is at 4 percent rate, twenty interviews on the average will see a person properly located. When 6 percent of the people are out of work, experience has shown that an average of thirty interviews will be required. Yes, it is a 50 percent increase in relative terms, but at the rate of one interview a day, which a well-planned campaign should generate, it is only ten extra days in absolute terms. There is one other difference: in times of low unemployment you can generally demand and command a much improved salary on making a change. This will usually not be the case in times of high unemployment, for companies and their executives, aware that they are in a purchasers' market, become cost conscious.

Concentrating on unemployment figures is a gloomy and unrewarding experience that inhibits action and ignores some constructive truths. Even if the unemployment rate is at 7 percent, we should not forget that this also means that 93 percent of the employable population is working, and that the largest market in good times and bad is provided by restlessness, which causes one person in five to change jobs every year. In 1970 at a time of high employment, close to 80 million people had jobs and 3 million were out of work; 17 million jobs changed hands in that year alone, which means that 3 million people were playing musical chairs with 1.5 million jobs each month. At a later time when 5.5 million people were out of work, they were playing musical chairs with 1.4 million jobs per month. If one doubles the speed of exposure, one has completely compensated for this difference in the job market.

Why do you want to switch your career?

This question may be asked in an interview and is easy to dispose of. You are not switching careers. Do not fall into the trap. You are seeking a new position, a new way to use your talents. If you are marketing or developing land or managing hotel conventions or travel associations or selling apples, you are always the same person with the same talents. It does not matter what the immediate problem is as long as your talents and experience can be brought to bear on a solution of the problem. A manager is a manager. This holds true of other capabilities unless the job requires advanced degrees or specialized knowledge which you do not have.

Why do you want to get into this field?

When this question is asked, many people regard it as hostile and immediately seek a thesis to explain the why. But if you think a bit, you will realize it is not a hostile question at all. It is not asked *against* you.

Let us see how it works. You enter an office for an interview with a man in a field which, unknown to you, is a bad one. The executive will announce that fact within a very few minutes. "We don't have anything open and, believe me, if I were you I wouldn't get into this field at all. Look at the way it's been going for the last five years. If I could get out myself I would."

The question "Why do you want to get into this field?" is an invitation for you to throw bouquets. Your executive has been in the field ten years and he wants to hear you say it is an exciting field, a wonderful field, and that, by implication, he must be a very smart man to be in it. He will feel smug. He recognized the potential of the field ten years ago, and now you give your confirmation of what a genius he is.

There is another thing. You must remember that certain

questions are asked out of complete idleness while an interviewer is thinking up a good question. These questions are smoke screens to conceal his real thinking. In any case, remember that no question — while you are dealing with a rational person — is ever asked *against* you.

Why did you leave your last job?
Why do you want to leave your job?

Forget everything negative. Do not say you are having trouble with your boss. That is not useful information. It is worse than that: it is negative and detrimental. You should speak only in the highest terms of your past or present employer and your past or present corporation. You might say you want to leave your job because you feel you could make far faster progress in a firm where the management structure was not so rigid. Or: "I am working in an area which does not particularly appeal to me."

The important truth here is this: Never be defensive. Be brief. Long explanations are always defensive.

Stand by your guns, if an interviewer comes back at you and says, "Oh come on now. I know you've put up with those same conditions 18 years — now why the sudden desire to change?"

A tough question with an easy answer: "Well, even a tortoise wakes up." Or: "Until recently, it has been exciting and I have progressed at a very rapid rate, but I don't see this rapid progress continuing."

Your interviewer will always accept you at your own assessment if you are brief, sincere, and to the point. Even the fact that you were fired — unless you were fired for robbing the till — is unimportant to your interviewer. You do not have to be defensive.

How long have you been out of work?

This question will never be asked in the major area of your market because you are asking for advice, not a job. It will not be asked because it is not a polite question. It may be asked if you apply for a job through an agency or a newspaper ad. The proper answer is: "I haven't been out of work. In fact, I've never been so busy, organizing my talents and trying to analyze where they could be of most service."

Do you feel you have the necessary technical knowledge?

"We would really like to hire you but you haven't had any experience in marketing fancy towels." You are, in general, required to have no more technical experience than that required for understanding marketing procedures. Technical information is available. If you are interested in the job, your answer would be:

"Well, I'm sure that with my background and versatility and the assistance I would get from the staff, I could master the necessary technical details in a short time."

Marketing is marketing. Managing is managing. Accounting is accounting whether you are accounting for redwood logs or sporting goods.

How much money are you making?
How much money do you want?
What is the minimum you will take to start?

Three questions but actually one, and in my opinion they come under the head of impertinent inquisitiveness.

If the question is put before you have been offered a job, your reply will be something like this, delivered with a smile: "Well, you know, I've always made it a principle never to discuss salary unless I am talking about an actual position. I'm sure you understand that." You have invited your interviewer to join the club of the good guys who understand or the fools who do not understand. He or she will always join the club which understands.

Another response to the question is equally valid. Talk about the future. "I'm looking for a position that can pay me twenty-five to thirty thousand in four or five years." Fine. Now everyone feels safe. You did not say he must pay you $30,000. You have told him you are ambitious and willing to work hard to achieve your goal.

Now what happens with someone who insists on knowing what your previous salary was or what you are currently making? About one in ten will insist. If you are helplessly trapped by such a fellow, your course is clear: Take your salary and add everything into it that you can — without lying. Put in the pension plan, Blue Cross, the life insurance, anything you can add legitimately and reply, "I estimate my job to be worth X number of dollars a year."

A job has been discussed and the inevitable question hangs in the air: "What are you making? How much do you want?" You say, "The job you describe sounds fascinating. I really feel I could turn in a good show on a job like that. I'm sure you have a perfectly fair salary structure, and I think the fairest thing to do would be to go along with your structure. How much did you have in mind?"

The question now hangs in the air. Your interviewer then will come back and say, "We had twenty thousand in mind." Or, if he thinks he is very, very shrewd, he will give you a range. "We had in mind anywhere from seventeen to twenty thousand." He will give you a range because he does not want to state an actual figure — yet it is clear he wants you with his firm. He is an executive and you know that the strength of an executive is that he is a decision maker. You know, also, that his weakness is that he makes decisions when he should not. When you say, "How much did you have in mind?" you tickle his decision-making muscle. About ninety-five times out of a hundred he will come back at you with a price or a range.

Your reaction is the same in each case. You repeat the single figure or the top figure of the range. Repeating it with a quizzically furrowed brow, you say, "Twenty thousand?" The question mark is the important thing. And then, even though your heart and head tell you to shout "Whoopie!" you put your head down and look at the floor. You are silent, pensive, and clearly discontented. You sulk. You say nothing.

As stated before, no one can remain silent for thirty seconds. It is true here and in nine cases out of ten he will mention another figure — at least 10 percent higher than the one you questioned. Why? Because he is making you an offer. In other words, he is a salesman, and there is only one thing a salesman cannot stand and that is a nonpurchasing look on a prospect's face. He will do everything within reason to wipe off that look. Furthermore, he did not give you an offer at the top of his range. He stated a figure which was the minimum reasonable amount he thought he could hire you for.

Your man has said twenty thousand, and you are in a sulk. He says, "Well, in view of your background, I may be able to go to twenty-three thousand."

You hesitate a few seconds and then look up as though you had not sulked at all. And you say, "The starting salary is certainly important, but it's not all-important. I'm concerned about the future. In six months' time, when you evaluate me, will it be on my demonstrated worth or will it just be a mechanical procedure?"

He has no choice but to reply, "On your demonstrated worth." Otherwise he admits that he is a thief, that you will get no more than a mechanical cost-of-living increase, regardless of your performance.

But suppose you repeat the top figure with a quizzical look and that vital question mark and go into a sulk and your man does not come up in price at all? He will begin to talk, about a company car, expense account, the great opportunity with the company, anything to sell you. At the proper moment, you raise your head and ask your question about the method of evaluating your performance. He might say, "We don't evaluate every six months at your level — at your level we evaluate annually." Fine, you think — because in most companies people at twenty thousand and up are evaluated only once a year.

You are excited and pleased but you remember Rule Number Seven: *Never accept or reject an offer while you are in the room,* and you say sincerely, "I certainly thank you very much for this offer and I am certainly very interested. When do you want my decision? I know you don't want me to say 'Yes' right now. I have to think it over. . . ."

Then get out of that office as fast as you can. If you were a client of mine, I would ask you to scurry right back to me to review the bidding and see what extras you may be entitled to: Car? Expense account? Moving expenses? Stock options? Consultant's fee? In pieces you can get quite a lot more than was discussed in the room. If you ask for these things right after a discussion of salary, your chances of getting them are very small.

Why do I advise you to mention only the top figure named? Here is a story which illustrates the reason. We had a client, a very fine man, who was very scholarly and also very shy. He had heard that his department was going to be eliminated for economy reasons. He was scared stiff.

He was making about $15,000, which was several thousand dollars under what he was worth. We worked carefully with him, but we were worried. We feared his timidity would lead him to flub any interview. Almost immediately, he was invited to be interviewed for a position which seemed ideal for him. He had a long interview and was delighted with the possibilities of the job.

Then came the crucial question. "How much are they paying you in your present job?"

"I was told that that's not a fair question," the client stuttered out. "I'm supposed to go by your structure or something like that. How much do you have in mind for the job?"

The interviewer said, "We thought anywhere from eighteen to twenty-four thousand."

The client flipped. "Eighteen thousand!" he cried—and he remembered he was supposed to sulk and not get so excited. He sulked.

So his man said, "All right, we can go to twenty thousand."

The client was now in bad shape. He could not remember what he was supposed to do at the end of the sulk, so he kept right on sulking.

His interviewer said, "All right, if we have to, we'll give you twenty-four."

Our client was overjoyed. He accepted the job immediately and came back to us in triumph.

It was a disaster. He lost his moving expenses, his consultant's fee, and all the rest. But still worse was the reaction of the man who had hired him. We are all infuriated if we think someone takes advantage of us. Now the new employer thinks, "Damn it, I was a fool. I got caught in that. The man was delighted with eighteen thousand. He'd probably been happy with fifteen and I got him at twenty-four." So by the time our client—who had not got all he was entitled to—showed up for work, he faced a boss who was already antagonistic toward him.

So go for the top figure and never accept or reject an offer while in the room with an interviewer. An offer can usually be improved by fringe benefits. An offer can be used as leverage with another firm you might prefer to work for.

Suppose you have been offered what seems an ideal position but the salary is too low. The proper procedure is to generate another offer that is better. Then you return to the first one, the one with the idea job, and you say, "I'm very interested in your job. I realize the job as it is presently described is not worth any more than the fifteen thousand you've mentioned. I thought, perhaps, that there might be a way of broadening the duties or changing the title so I could take a job with you at my real market value. I have been offered twenty thousand by the ABC Company, but I would much rather work for you if we can get together."

Salary, of course, is very important. And that is why I advise you to go as high as possible up the executive ladder in your market campaign. It will not always be possible to see presidents of firms or even vice presidents—but *as a practical matter you should never be interviewed except by persons at least two notches above your own level.* You do not want to be interviewed by the one for whom you will work—your interviewer must always be above that level. If you want to work for a vice president, get advice and counsel and make a favorable impression on the president. If you are to work under a foreman, get an interview with the foreman's department head.

Another very practical reason for shooting high is that it does no good to be interviewed by someone making $20,000 a year when your goal is $30,000. Such a person could not afford to be generous. But if a vice president making $75,000 a year wants you, he or she is not going to haggle over one or two thousand. A thousand dollars viewed from $75,000 a year is not the same as a thousand viewed from $20,000 a year.

A final reason, paramount in importance: Maximum pay means maximum respect, and all that follows in your job is affected by your initial salary.

How do you handle the stress interview?

A stress interview—no longer as popular as it once was and very unlikely to occur as you seek advice and counsel in the unpublished section of the job market—is designed to make you lose your temper. Your interviewer or interviewers—sometimes they double up to make you uncomfortable—ask foolish questions. They might give you a cigar but provide no ashtray; they might seat you on a chair with uneven legs so that you teeter back and forth; they might sit obliquely from you so you must squirm in your chair to see them face to face; one might question you while another takes pictures of you. They want to find out at what point you will break.

It is a silly procedure, but you must be prepared if some idiot tries it on you. As regards foolish or maddening questions: You will not answer any question which you consider inappropriate, an invasion of your privacy, irrelevant, or deliberately trivial. You handle the situation with controlled humor. You smile and say, "That's a good question. Just how am I supposed to answer it?"

Since the whole idea of the stress interview is to rattle you, get you off balance, make you lose your temper, you conquer if you keep calm. Even an interviewer following a step-by-step stress interview plan will lose faith in the procedure if you can keep calm for ten minutes or so.

If you are given a cigar with no ashtray, ask politely for an ashtray. If your chair rocks from side to side, ask for another chair. If your interviewer seats himself in an awkward position for you, move your chair—out into the corridor, if necessary—and explain, "My mother always said I must see the person I am talking to."

Sometimes hostile questioning may have some point. I remember one case in which our client was a financial planner and everything on his résumé indicated that fact. He was called in by a financial vice president who read his résumé and said, "Well, you know, Mr. So-and-so, we're really looking for a financial planner, someone with financial planning experience."

Our client bristled. "Look at my résumé. There is nothing

there that isn't financial planning. My whole experience has been financial planning."

The vice president flicked the résumé and said, "Mr. So-and-so, do you really call this financial planning?"

"Do you really call this an interview?" said our client.

"Not if you don't want to call it an interview," said the vice president. "And now I say 'Good-bye' to you."

Our man was furious and also very downcast, because he had very much wanted the position. A few days later, he received a letter from the mean vice president.

"Dear Mr. So-and-so: You are eminently qualified for the position we had to offer. You have not, however, learned to master your emotions to the degree that would be required in the job we had. It is a very frustrating job with many people to aggravate you fifty times a day. I hope that with some attention in this area, you will eventually occupy positions far greater than this one."

What are your weaknesses?

At about one interview in ten you will hear that question. "You've told me all about how wonderful you are, but what are your weaknesses? I want to know what's wrong with you."

Your response to such a question is to sit quietly pondering the question for a minute or two. Then you say, "I guess it would be a weakness to take a position which did not use my talents properly, and I'm not foolish enough to do that."

But perhaps the interviewer, who is in a bad mood, will not accept that. "Oh, come now. No one's perfect. You've got to have some weaknesses."

"Well, of course," you reply, "I have weaknesses, I suppose. I just don't pay too much attention to them. I'm certain any weaknesses I have would not affect the execution of my job."

You do not have to be deadly serious all the time. Quiet humor is a wonderful tool. It keeps the atmosphere friendly and pleasant:

Interviewer: *You've got to have some weaknesses. What's the worst thing you ever did in your life?*

You (with a smile): *Gee, I'd never put a thing like that in print.*

When should you pull strings?

Never try to pull strings or have pressure exerted from the outside. It almost never works for you and can always work against you.

Why do you want to work here?

Another gentle question. Your interviewer wants to hear some soft music. If you can say it sincerely, say, "I've been impressed by the public reports about your company. I think your industry is fascinating and I admire your organization. As a matter of fact, my impressions have been confirmed by the attitudes you've taken in this interview. Rationally and intuitively, I feel this is a place I'd like to work."

Will your interviewer agree? Of course. She is employed by a fine company and she is a fine woman.

Here is another answer: "You've been talking with me, very thoughtfully and helpfully, for an hour. And if you want the truth, you're the kind of person I want to work for. An ideal job, I believe, would be to work as an assistant to someone like you."

That is a very large compliment, and compliments are hard to resist. If you can say such a thing honestly, say it.

I will round off this discussion with three more points and then I will state a prime rule.

Certain companies may send you to a psychiatrist for an examination. You have nothing to worry about. The psychiatrist knows nothing about the job you have been offered. He knows nothing about you. He will respond to you as any other human being. If you are nice to him he will be nice to you. Your role is to be relaxed, be yourself, and let him feel he is earning the four hundred dollars he will charge the firm. The psychiatrist will give a good report because he does not wish to antagonize you. He knows that, if he does, you may someday be in a position to retaliate. You have nothing to worry about unless you are tense when you approach such an examination.

Many companies, on hiring people, especially for higher positions, arrange meetings with both the candidate and his wife or her husband before making a final offer. People in general interpret these interviews as being an evaluation of the candidate's partner. This is rarely if ever the case. The purpose of such interviews is to sell the company to the candidate's partner and thereby add a powerful advocate in promoting the desired association.

Some companies use "family-type interviews." You will be sent to meet the controller and the auditor and the traffic manager and so on until you are dizzy. These people are being exposed to you through these little interviews because you will have to cooperate with them once you are on the job. The person hiring you wants to feel they have had a hand in blessing your arrival — so they cannot pull the rug out from under you when you report for work. Your general rule of being courteous and pleasant and otherwise keeping your mouth shut will work well for you in such family interviews. The bright youngster delegated to introduce you to these others is your only foe. He is there to observe your reactions and your mistakes. Your rule holds for him, too: courtesy and a closed mouth.

Now for the prime rule: *Never answer any serious question off the top of your head.*

Let me give you an example. My secretary comes in and says, "Mr. Djeddah, the dog's fallen down the lavatory. What shall I do?"

I answer off the top of my head. "Pull the plug. Call the police department. Call the dog catcher." I have to take action. I have only a few minutes to make up my mind and I give a quick answer.

But suppose an associate came into me and said, "Eli, we're going to open twenty new branches and I want you to handle it." Would I leap from my desk and shout, "We ought to open in Seattle and Chicago and we ought to be in Timbuktu and ..."? Of course not. Such a program would demand a great deal of thought, and I would be a fool to answer it off the top of my head.

We had a client who was one of three candidates for an important job. After several interviews, the president of the firm called him in.

"We have a problem," the president said. "We have three wonderful candidates for this job and we are having a difficult time choosing the right one. So I am seeing all three of you individually and then we will make up our minds.

"The real crux of the matter is that we have acquired nine small corporations in the last couple of years and our main concern and the main responsibility of the individual we hire will be to coordinate, synchronize, and hybridize the cash flow, the reporting methods, and the accounting procedures — to make sense out of what are nine unrelated activities."

"Yes," said our client. "Your financial people have explained that."

"Well," said the president, "what I'd really like to know is how you would propose to solve the problem."

The client was well trained — "Never answer any serious question off the top of your head" — and he said, "Well, I'm a little embarrassed. I simply can't answer now. I think I would need several weeks and probably several months to accumulate all the information I'd need to come up with probable answers."

While he talked, the president raised himself by the arms of his chair, smiling like a baby. Two days later, our client was hired. When he had been in harness a few weeks he learned the president had also put his question to the two other candidates, who had "solved" the problem in five minutes. Solved the problem the president himself had been working on for eight months. Even if their solutions had been right, they were insulting the intelligence of the president.

People respect you for being sensible. *Never answer any serious question off the top of your head.*

12 The Internal Campaign—and Method Number Twelve

I promised to outline twelve ways of getting a job, and we have covered eleven methods in the published and unpublished sections of the job market. The twelfth way of getting a job is to tend the vegetables in your own backyard—to improve your position within your present company. In our counseling we see the necessity of a campaign to improve conditions internally in two situations. In the first, someone comes in fearful of losing his or her job and anxious to get out and look for another before the blow falls. In the second, an individual asks for counsel because of a feeling of being boxed in and wanting to accelerate his or her progress within a company.

The signs of how you are doing on a job are easy to read. When you are on your way up, your duties are broadened, your title is changed, and you are rewarded financially. When you are on the way out, your duties are narrowed, your title is diminished, and your pay is reduced.

A person who is employed comes in to us because he is unhappy with his job. He recognizes he has a problem he is unable to solve by himself and realizes he needs help. First, we have to face one of the harsh realities of life: that in any area of unsolved problems, we all regress to an emotional level. When you are emotional, your world becomes a world of people only, a world in which you blame people for their actions, fear them, try to retaliate. "Damn my boss. He's always after me. He's riding me. He's going to fire me."

Now, because you are emotionally involved you have cut off communication with your superior. You must recall that you got the job in the first place because you were expected to be useful in your superior's complex of problems. Your usefulness is dependent on flying consistently on the radar beam of communication between you and your boss. When you turn off this communication, you begin to diverge from the radar beam, the true course, and as time passes the divergence becomes greater and greater. You are on a negative trend.

Or say you are performing some service for your boss. He is happy with your work but you can see no sign of progress. Because you can see no progress, you feel rejected. So while the boss may be happy with your work, he is not delighted, quite possibly because your feeling of being rejected is putting a crimp in your efficiency a bit, draining away some of your energy. You do not communicate with your boss because you dare not.

There is a third situation. When someone seeks counseling while still employed, he sometimes suffers from a feeling of guilt. He has the feeling he is going behind his boss's back and he begins to rationalize his action. The easiest way to rationalize in this situation is to generate more animosity toward his boss or his firm. So the very decision to look for a job or to seek counseling may compound your problem by guilt and the rationalization of guilt.

These situations really constitute one over-all problem. The first thing we do with our clients is to make sure they do not lose their jobs in the middle of counseling: we want to know the donkey is secure while we are looking for the horse. To ensure that an individual does not lose his or her job, we put the client on an immediate internal campaign, showing ways to make the job secure. We want the client to feel free of guilt — and you will be guilt-free whenever you are doing a good job.

Another thing. Who gets offers of jobs, Dismal Desmond or Jovial Joe? We turn our clients into Jovial Joes. This can be done the minute they feel they are doing a good job, a fine job, where they are employed. When they feel they are accomplishing tremendously, they feel secure, free of guilt, and very ambitious. We show them how to *move* into a new situation and not run to one. Moving consists of having choices: the choice to stay with the present company or the choice to move.

An internal campaign is really a simple thing. It consists of generating merit and communicating with your superior. How is this done? You define a problem which is not directly in your area of responsibility. You go to your boss and say, "Boss, I think it might be a good idea to work on this problem." The boss looks at your proposal, recognizes the possibility of an extra dividend, and gives you the go-ahead. You work out the problem and come up with a solution. Boss is pleased. Pick another problem and go back to your boss. "Boss, the first problem worked out so well, I'm now working on this one." Boss has two choices, tell you to forget the whole thing — that the building is falling down and the main job is to prop it up, or agree that you tackle your second self-discovered problem.

After you have been through a few of these problems and come up with solutions, your attitude will be bound to improve. Your boss likes you very much. He talks to you all the time — he is communicating — and you know what is on his mind. You know you are on the beam again and you know how to serve him. Three things: you are earning your money; you have made your job secure; you are free of guilt. In a word, you are Jovial Joe. You are now in a position to get offers from the outside.

More than that, you are in a position to move up within your own firm. You go to your boss just before periodic raises are due.

You say, "Will you evaluate me on the basis of my demonstrated worth and not on a mechanical principle?" The boss has no choice but to agree to evaluate you on your demonstrated merit. Otherwise, he will have to say to himself, "I am a thief so I will give a mechanical raise." No one likes to admit to being a thief.

Now the time for the annual increases rolls around. The boss has $5,000 to spread around and he has always made a mechanical five-way split — $1,000 to each employee. With you in mind, he says, "I can't give him a mere one thousand — I can't get away with that after I told him he would be evaluated on merit. I'll give him two thousand. He's certainly worth that." Now, once this decision is made, one or more of the other four involved is going to get hurt. You may have hurt a fellow worker but you have secured your own job. Say your boss gives you $2,000 and three others the mechanical $1,000. When he gets to the fifth person, he has nothing left to give. Perhaps he could split up one of the $1,000 raises — $600 to the fourth person and $400 to the fifth. This, he realizes, is an insult. To justify it, he asks himself, "Is that guy really worth any raise? He came in late Monday morning. Tuesday he turned in a sloppy report and Wednesday he had the effrontery to make a mistake." He forgets the man came in Saturday for some special work. He forgets the man has been doing a good job for many years. He has to find a reason for not giving him even the mechanical raise, and the low man is doomed.

Then he begins to think, "Did I give So-and-so two thousand because he was worth it or did he force me into it?" The answer is simple and quick. "Nothing is ever forced out of me. So-and-so's been working like a trooper; the only one with initiative around here." You and the boss are in a positive atmosphere, and even while he is thinking his long thoughts, you are doing everything you can to please him. The poor man at the end of the line does not know what has hit him. He feels the boss's eye on him all the time. He begins to hate his boss — he becomes emotional and gives the boss more proof of his own rightness. The following year, the boss may very well be ready to fire the poor fellow. Meanwhile, because you are on a positive trend with your boss, you will get a raise larger than anyone else the next time around.

We have just gone through a theoretical—though exactly true—case. Now, how do you put yourself in this position? A moment's thought will show you the way; fortunately for you no one else is likely to take time for a moment's thought.

The first thing to do when you begin your course of improvement is to pay your company the compliment of finding out what it is engaged in—what its purpose is and how it goes about implementing that purpose. This may seem like a strange piece of advice, but you would be amazed to know how many people spend their entire working lives hardly aware of the business their firm is engaged in.

There are many ways to get to know your company. Read its annual report. Read its balance sheet. Read its news releases. Read stock market studies. Senior officers and executives can give you a vast knowledge of the company you work for, providing your interest is sincere. Interest is the guide. We acquire knowledge only when we are sensitized in a certain area. Then we invariably find out endless new things because we are attuned. While we are interested, knowledge is ours.

When you know something about the nature of your company, find out as much as you can about your own department. Where does it fit in the corporate structure? What is its importance in the over-all picture? You will find that the company does not necessarily consider your department the center of its activities. Learn how your work meshes with the rest of the organization. Your source of this information is your direct superior. Your search for knowledge gives you an opportunity to talk to your boss because he knows more than you do. He is expected to know more.

When you have determined what business your company is in and where your department fits in the over-all picture, find out where you fit in your department. If you are in a line position, sit down and write out a list of your responsibilities, however well you think you know them. Take your sheet of paper to your boss and say, "Boss, I want to check with you. Here is my view of my job and my responsibilities." You will be surprised, perhaps shocked, by the boss's response. Some of the responsibilities you have assumed will come as a complete surprise to him. He will strike some from your list, but, you can be sure, he will indicate many others he has abdicated to you without your knowledge. Together you can define your job clearly—and establish lines of communication at the same time.

Then go through the pleasant exercise of asking the people who report to you to write down a description of what they think their job is, no matter how menial that job may be. At the same time, play a game of blind man's buff with them: write out your own list of their responsibilities. When you place both sheets together you will have to go into a mini-Moses conference at the top of the mount to reconcile the two lists. But when the lists are in agreement, and the process has been repeated for your whole staff, you will have set the stage for an effective organization. You yourself can grow only in a frame of reference which is growing. You can grow only in an activity which is growing. The people under you can grow only when you grow.

Here again, we return to the necessity of effective planning. What is planning? It is the setting of goals, humble though they may be, and naming a road to those goals, however doubtful the road may be, and then dividing the road into the number of steps necessary to reach the goals.

One of the greatest difficulties faced by anyone is translating thought into action. There is a tremendous waste of time in internal dialogue and purposeless hesitation. A machine that spins around endlessly without producing anything is very busy, but its output is zero. A mind that thinks backward and forward all day may produce nothing. We need organization.

Your effectiveness could be increased immeasurably if you could reduce the agonizing pause between making decisions and taking action. Planning—not just goal setting but naming a road and designating the steps up the road to the goal—is a simple way to get relief from this problem. It has several advantages. One, you will not have to re-examine constantly. I have a good memory. The result is that I think of the twenty things I have to do fifty times a day unless I write those twenty things down on paper, with a note of the time of day each will be faced. Thus, I eliminate them from my mind and do them one by one as they come up.

If it is your job as manager to plan the workday of the people under you, you must realize that no one but you can plan your own day's work. Planning teaches you to be a self-motivator. When you set your goals and lay out a program to reach them, you can multiply your free hours. If in eight hours you could increase your output 20 percent, you would have 20 percent more time to rest or to play or to earn more money.

Planning and organizing does something else of an even profounder nature: it is an exercise in self-discipline. As William Penn said, "No man is fit to command another that cannot command himself." If you are in control of yourself, if you can plan for yourself as well as others, if you can organize yourself, if you can condition yourself to do the things you say you will do and do them at the planned time, then you can indeed become a powerful person. You can direct your powers and energies in any direction you choose.

When I speak of knowing your company and your department, and stress the necessity for planning and structuring your job, your response may be, "Anyone knows how to define and structure a line position. All you have to do is go up to personnel and get one of their volumes for that. But I'm not one of those people: I am on the staff, which means that I am forever drifting off on little clouds where no one can define me. My security lies in nondefinition."

To that I say, "Absolute bunk. There is no difference between a staff position and a line job if you structure your staff job properly."

And you reply, "All right. I have a staff position. How can I structure my position so I will have the security and the same sense of meaning as someone in a line job?"

I have suggested that you inform yourself about your company, your department, and the department's place in the company. One of my colleagues is fond of quoting a little plaque that hangs on many walls. It begins something like this: "If you work for a man, for heaven's sake work for him. . . ." It behooves you to know your man, because only by knowing him can you really benefit him and thereby benefit the over-all purpose of your company. By the steps I have suggested, you and your boss can define your job. You will find this a delightful experience because, once it is done, you will be one of a very few people who know exactly what you are doing and what your job is. Now, once you know your role, you can go around, as suggested, and chat with your co-workers. Discover what picture they have of themselves and their jobs. When you have classified this information, you will discover there are unfilled responsibilities all around you — and the pleasing opportunity to enrich yourself quite honestly and justly. You can locate uninhabited islands of responsibility and delegate them to yourself. You can expand your own responsibilities. Knowing a situation, defining its needs, may enable you to come up with a new job description so beneficial to the organization that you can create a new position — a new title for yourself.

Once again, I hear your disappointed voice. "You make it sound simple, but I'm in a company which is absolutely rigid." Or, "I work for the city and I could never create a new job." I say that such expressions are a willful acceptance of defeat. Further, I say that you can almost always sell something which is in the interest of your superiors. In a highly structured organization such as the military, it is simple — and done many times — for a man to wring his hands and moan, "I can only progress at such and such a pace and I might as well accept it." More junk. Two men start out as second lieutenants. One retires as a major, the other retires as a general. What was the difference? They both lived in the same highly structured world, but one went farther than the other.

Progress can be made in any organization — in one as highly structured as the country's largest companies, which always seem to go by the rule book; even in the military. Take positive action and make sure your contributions are known and recognized by your superior. If you are in proper communication with him, he will repay you because it is human nature to pay a debt. Know your boss, know how he operates, and work at your very best level to help.

In this area of creating positions, you cannot make progress by killing off your superiors in the hope of occupying their chairs. It is only in a growing situation that you can grow. It is by pushing someone who is ahead of you along by assisting him that you can fill his seat when he is promoted.

When entering a new firm or taking a different job with your own company, the first condition is humility—recognize that you are not a god or a demigod. We all have the feeling that the whole world revolves around our splendid persons, so we take any new position with every good intention to improve things. Here I remind you only that the road to hell is paved with such intentions.

I remember my reaction one time I started a new job. "What can I do for these people? They have called on me, this unique genius, to right all the things that are wrong." With relentless speed—there is nothing more dangerous than a busy fool—I started to churn around and investigate all areas of my new firm. I made rapid estimates—guesstimates—and intuitive decisions of all sorts. I found out there were thousands of things wrong. I was looking for faults, and every fault I found was a validation of my presence on the scene, a confirmation of the genius of the one who hired me and an ego boost for me. For weeks on end, I had a merry time. I wrote little reports to the president, I issued commands and edicts—and I had everyone in turmoil.

You can well imagine how many friends I made. I could have written the antithesis to Dale Carnegie: *How to Win Enemies and Ensure Your Own Defeat.* There is a truth here: No matter how right you are in your decision, every time you are right you have invalidated someone else. And you are hardly likely to be right all the time. That would be very tedious and you would become bored with yourself. Also it would be audacious and incautious to believe that any company which has been in business a long time could have survived by knowing nothing of its own business. Management does know a few things. Management might be antiquated and it might be slow, but enough is known so the company survives. Management was at least prosperous enough to hire you. Inevitably some of your early inspirations — generated by energy and conceit — will be completely wrong. Some of them will have been tried and found ineffective ten or fifteen years before. Others will be nullified by factors you are unaware of.

But I paid no attention to such things. I pursued my own course with relentless energy. I overlooked the great truth that if you do not make friends you make enemies, and in the space of about thirty days, being a very active man, working about sixteen hours a day, thinking about twelve times faster than the average person — multiply the factors involved — I made about two thousand more errors than the average person. A lazy man would have been secure. With all my energy and ideas, I was winning enemies on all sides. In the end, a pygmy armed with a toothpick, a pygmy I had not even suspected, got to my jugular vein. He never forgot and he never forgave. He was waiting to repay an eye for an eye and a tooth for a tooth and he got both my eyes and all my teeth and I was out of a job.

Human relations are important. You cannot improve your position if everyone dislikes you.

The first thing to do on entering a new position is to observe quietly, question gently, and listen. You will have many ideas. Write them on little cards. Put the cards in a box by your bed. When the mood takes you, read them, discarding the ones which have soured as you go. After thirty days, the cards that remain may be worth including in a report to your superiors. Write the report and let it age for thirty days. The Romans had a saying, *festina lente* — hasten slowly. There is always time to present the brilliant thoughts you have wrenched from your genius, imagination, and experience. If an idea is right, it will be right for many years. It can incubate under the critical eye of examination and re-examination before you announce it to the world.

Once you have put yourself into a positive situation vis-à-vis your boss, you are in an excellent position to begin a market campaign inside your own firm. Either before or just after you have received a raise, based on your performance, write a nice letter to your boss, a letter containing the essence of the résumé you have devised. Let the letter speak of your accomplishments and indicate a goal. You write, "I would really like to talk to you.

Where am I going in this firm? I am ambitious, as you know." You have a pleasant conversation with your boss. He is happy with you because he has either just given you a bribe in the form of a raise or is about to. He may very well give you a glowing prediction as to your future with the firm.

This is the time to go into the external market and generate an offer. With offer in hand, you again visit your boss. This time you say, "Boss, I have problems. They are soliciting me. I've been offered thirty thousand a year and I'm a very unhappy person, because you know how much I love this company and how I would hate to leave."

You have elegantly reversed roles. Had you gone to your boss to announce an offer out of the blue, his reaction would have been like something out of Alice in Wonderland: "Treason! Traitor! Off with his head!" But instead, the boss now feels guilty and a little foolish. He thinks, "I should have known when I talked to him last month. I should have given him a bigger raise or enlarged his responsibilities." Aloud he says, "Calm down. Only yesterday I was talking to the vice president about you. There is a whole new set of plans emerging. Can you hold your horses for a few days!" Now he is really talking business, because you have a loaded gun in your pocket. Alternatively, if your boss does not react in this way, you have an offer and can move.

I'll round out this chapter with an example of an internal campaign taken from my files. J.L. was the client, a lovely, very competent man, a certified public accountant with a top scholastic record and high degrees. He worked for a security analyst's firm as assistant controller at thirteen thousand a year. He reported to the controller of the firm. The controller reported to the president and to the treasurer. The treasurer retired and the controller was moved into his spot. J.L. was given the responsibilities of the controller—along with his other duties—but not the title or the money he deserved.

That was the situation when he arrived at my office. He was a painfully shy man, too shy to go out on interviews, so the only course was to work within his own company. But we could not mount a strong internal campaign because J.L. was simply unable to take the proper steps—another reflection of his shyness. I called his wife.

"You are a lovely lady," I said, "but I've grown to dislike you. In fact, I hate you."

"Why? What's wrong?"

"You're cheating me. You promised you would nag and make life unbearable for J.L. until he got into action. It's a criminal shame that he is being exploited so. You've got to help me."

"Aye, aye, Captain," she said. "What do I do?"

"Nag him until he will make a move in self-defense," I said.

The next time I saw the client, I said, "J.L., your wife thinks I'm a thief. She thinks I took your money under false pretenses because you're not getting anywhere on your job. Naturally, she blames me."

"Okay," said J.L. "I'm sick and tired of hearing about it. What should I do?"

We wrote a letter to the president of the firm. We cited all the things J.L. had done and asked the president for an opportunity to discuss things with him. J.L. wrote that he did not know where he was delinquent, but the fact was that for a year and a half he had been performing very heavy duties and had somehow failed to be recognized for his work. He said he was worried and beginning to wonder if he should stay with the company.

In other words, he had performed his job well but his communications were bad. His letter was an attempt to open up lines of communication and to bring his accomplishments to the president's attention.

The president, a stiff and stern New Englander, pretended he did not receive the letter. There was nothing but silence from his austere office. J.L. came to me, shyer than ever and feeling he had made a presumptuous mistake.

"What can I do now?"

"Let him digest the letter for a while," I said. "He has to answer it."

"But it's been two months."

"We've pointed out the facts of your situation," I said. "Under the circumstances, he must increase your salary because he is not a thief. We'll wait until you get a raise and then really start to move. Believe me—take me on faith."

After another month of silence, J.L. was summoned into the president's office. "J.L.," he said, "you have been doing a very good job. We're happy with your work and we're going to give you a very substantial increase in salary—three thousand, to be exact."

Three thousand dollars was an immense amount at that firm. I had never heard of such a raise there. J.L. was delighted, of course. He sent me a letter saying every member of the board of directors had congratulated him and the whole firm was buzzing about the fat raise. "I've never been treated with such respect."

I asked him to come to see me. When he came in, I said, "Now we have to move."

"I can't," J.L. said. "It would be indecent after they've given me such a raise."

"Indecent or not, we're going to push a little harder. It's better to blush for a moment than be pale all your life. I want you to go to the treasurer and say something like this: 'Mr. Treasurer, I have a very serious problem. I was not too concerned about my salary, and you know I have received a very handsome raise. But I am unhappy because I do not feel you think I am adequate for my job. Since I have been doing the controller's work, plus my own as assistant controller, for a year and a half, I wondered why I was not made controller. Then, this morning, my wife said, "J.L., you're an awful fool. You're reporting to two people and you are assuming that each one knows your problem. It is more than likely that the president and the treasurer each assumes that the other has taken care of you. In the meantime, you're lost in the middle." I think she is right, Mr. Treasurer, and I plead guilty to very bad communication. Can you help me correct my communication? I want the dignity and title of my position.' "

J.L.—at what cost to his shy nature no one will ever know—acted out the little drama sketched above. The treasurer said, "Okay, J.L., I'll take it up with the president."

Several days later the president called J.L. in "J.L.," he said, "I'm not going to be pushed on this matter. I'm damned if I'll make you controller until the annual meeting. But we will pay you for having waited. When we name you controller, we'll give you another three thousand increase."

It is a fact that people value investments, perhaps over-value them. The president had invested $3,000 in J.L. and J.L. was a more valuable man in his eyes for it.

I repeat: The signs of how you are operating in your job are easy to read. When you are on your way up, your duties are broadened, your title is changed, and you are rewarded financially. When you are on the way out, your duties are narrowed, your title is diminished, and your pay is reduced.

As an afterthought, I leave this idea with you. If things are going badly in your job and you feel certain you are about to be fired, think a little about the future. While still employed, borrow three months' salary from a bank and put it in a savings account. Even if you have to pay 18 percent interest, your savings account will return you 7 percent—and a cost of 7 percent is very cheap insurance for a nest egg you may need during your market campaign. Once you are out of a job, very few banks will lend you money.

13 Handling Your Business Contacts

The power of courtesy is as limitless as the areas in which it operates. You will notice that I talk about it a lot — the thank-you letter, the effects of courtesy on receptionists, secretaries, switchboard operators. These are all practical considerations that will help you in your job campaign. And although it is my personal belief that courtesy must stem from a deep faith in people, from the realization that we belong to the rest of humanity and that the world is one, it is not my intention here to discuss with you the ethical or moral values of a do-unto-others approach to life. Very possibly you feel these values as deeply as I do, and in that case the natural grace of your actions will operate in your favor in every situation. Very likely, without any conscious effort, you exhibit a friendly respect toward everyone you encounter — which is, after all, what courtesy is all about — and you need no practical justification for doing so.

But we are talking of practical common-sense approaches to your job campaign, and it is important to stress the uses of courtesy in that context. To the degree that we all aspire to be loved, wanted, needed [*add here:* by a potential employer], it is in our deepest interest to have the whole world [*translation here:* the people who can help us toward the job we want] friendly to us. Courtesy opens doors. Courtesy begets courtesy. If you give it, you receive it.

Inherent in the idea of courtesy is dignity—by courteous acts you are respecting another's dignity and, equally important, demonstrating your own. The difference between being courteous and obsequious is very real. Courtesy in itself knows no rank. The attitude to adopt as you launch yourself into the market is that all people are potential friends, associates, cooperators, whether they are several levels above you in the corporate hierarchy or several levels below—and in fact the lower the rank of a person you deal with, the greater your concern should be, because to that person the difference in power may seem awesome and threatening.

But no matter what it is—practical considerations or natural goodwill—that normally moves you to do the courteous thing, at certain times during your job campaign you may have a tendency to omit courtesies you normally would never overlook. This is possible particularly in the very beginning when you are under strain, before you have gotten into the swing of going calmly to your interviews, confident of handling whatever comes up. Under such conditions you may be overly preoccupied with reacting mentally to what has taken place, and you may neglect to register your appreciation, say, of an exceptionally generous offer of help you have been given. So it pays to flex those muscles of courtesy regularly, in every area of your life, to ensure that they will be in good working order, ready to go into action whenever they appropriately should.

There are a number of miscellaneous questions that touch on matters of courtesy directly or indirectly. Some of them relate to your job campaign, others to your everyday business conduct. One concerns setting up your plans to see people. In all cases, when calling on anyone—referrals, friends, agencies, consulting firms—it is necessary to make appointments in advance and keep them promptly. You will notice that the inherent quality of courtesy—dignity—is involved here. You are granting other people dignity by assuming they lead orderly, busy working lives; you are also putting yourself in a position of dignity by prearranging your arrival. Few people welcome the person straggling in off the sidewalk. The late arrival is as repugnant as the guest who overstays his welcome. And bear in mind too that no one forgives an uncanceled broken appointment.

Courteous business letters are as important as courteous face-to-face encounters. You may find it valuable to study a good book of business letters. You will not necessarily want to parrot the precise style in which they are written, but you will absorb the general tone by simple exposure to them and adapt them naturally to your own style.

Striking deviations in dress in your job surroundings may seem to be an expression of hostility to those around you—the ones who can help or hurt you. If you wear a beard in a beardless world, a hat in a hatless world, theatrical makeup in a world of fresh-washed faces, skirts scarcely below the navel when the rest are at mid-calf, you do so at your own risk. In some areas, variety in dress styles is the rule and the problem does not exist. But otherwise it is a good idea when in Rome to do as the Romans do.

Have a drink at lunch?

The answer to this question, which may seem pretty removed from matters of courtesy, can pertain to your general comportment, your mental alertness, and the impression you create, so it belongs in this discussion.

I do not dare suggest what you do when you lunch with friends. I do care what you do at lunch when you are on a market campaign, and I herewith issue an edict: You will not drink if you are invited out to lunch by a prospective employer, though there be martinis to the right of you, highballs to the left of you, and bloody marys in front of you. Even if the prospective employer and others at the table order drinks, you are advised to say, "I think I'll have tomato juice today," or some other polite answer which will keep you away from alcohol.

Who pays for lunch?

When you lunch with business associates without specific invitation, the proper procedure is to go Dutch and divide the check. You eat out of your plate, not out of your associates' pockets. If you are a woman lunching informally with male colleagues, you still assume you will pay your share.

When you are the host at luncheon or dinner, you should give the order for all your guests. Very few people do this in the United States, and yet it is one of the most refined attentions you can pay your guests. Inquire what they would like in order of precedence — the most important lady first, the other women and girls in order of importance, then the most important man and on down the line. This little air of taking command of the table and your guests gives them a feeling of ease and gives the waiter notice as to who is host.

How to end an interview

If you are on the receiving end of a job application and have decided a candidate is unsatisfactory, you should say, "We have many applicants for the position we have discussed. Some of them have had the benefit of far longer experience and specific application that you have. I think you have an interesting background and I think you will do well in this field. But I think you will have to bide your time." You may be able to suggest that the applicant talk to someone. Be sincere and frank but try to help if you can.

A businesswoman of my acquaintance swears by her own method of concluding an interview. It is done without a word, entirely by body language. While the interview is in progress she sits back in her chair in a relaxed fashion, giving her full attention to the applicant across the desk. When she wants it to end she does not in any way drop her attentiveness but she changes her posture: she straightens up and moves into position over her desk. This simple gesture, merely hinting that she must now get back to work, almost invariably works for her, and her visitor takes leave as if she had said aloud, "It's time for you to go."

In informal situations, less tact is called for. If a small group has gathered in your office and you would like them to leave, simply say, "Look, I've got work to do." You do not have to put up with a lot of nonsense. If a group of your superiors is in the room, ask, "Can you tell me how much longer you will be? I have an appointment scheduled."

The role of small talk in business encounters

There seems to be an unwritten law that if you are lunching with someone for the purpose of talking business, you talk small talk first. The more crucial the business conversation is to be, the more important it is to talk for a while of anything but. By mutual unspoken agreement you are putting each other at ease, setting up a rapport, indirectly feeling each other out. If you are a job applicant talking to your prospective employer, you let him decide—even as late as over coffee and dessert—when to get into the subject that is on both your minds. You take your cue from him. But in any relationship—two people who want to discuss a business deal, boss and assistant tackling a knotty office problem, and so on—the chief point to remember is to be sensitive in terms of timing and to defer to the choice of the person whom the circumstances have placed in the driver's seat.

Traveling with business colleagues

Plane or train trips to appointments, meetings, or conventions consume many hours of many business people's lives. It is important to know that they use those hours for a number of purposes other than constant conversation with their accompanying colleagues. They may want simply to rest in preparation for the work to come. They may want to read. They may want to think out the role they are to play at their destination. Or, in the course of the trip, they may want to do all three. Here is another area requiring sensitivity to your companion's needs and desires. If he shows quite clearly that he wants no talk—if he opens his briefcase or leans back in his seat in a position of total rest or gives monosyllabic answers when you speak to him—stop talking. If there is urgent discussion to be had before you go into a meeting awaiting you at the other end, you may be sure he will allot the time for it before you arrive. Often it is the final leg of the trip that will be given to the necessary discussion.

Entertaining business associates at home

I am frequently asked by married men if their wives should entertain their business associates. I think a wife should be ready to do this if her husband wishes it. What should her attitude be—friendly or formal? She can be friendly without tumbling into people's arms; she can be poised without being frozen. She should never be obsequious. Neither should her attitude suggest, "I'm doing this only because I was forced into it." Above all, she should be a thoughtful hostess, just as she is with friends who come to dinner—and this means making her guests comfortable.

If it is your boss who has come to dinner, his or her comfort may be less than complete if, when shop talk comes up, your spouse takes an active part in the conversation, suggesting that you have told everything you know about everyone and everything that goes on at the office. A better choice is for your spouse to be a good listener and keep his or her own counsel. To some bosses all spouses are security risks. So flattering attentiveness and silence are the best course when the conversation turns to business.

flattering attentiveness and silence are her best course when the conversation turns to business.

A final note: The miscellaneous situations I have described here concern only a handful of common questions that will come up all the time in a person's working life, and my comments on them are not intended to suggest rigid rules of conduct. If your own actions always are based on readiness to consider how the other person feels, you can do what comes naturally to you and the chances are you will do the right thing.

14   A Word About Spouses

In this chapter I will discuss the role of the spouse of a person who is out of a job. The techniques and situations I have described thus far in the book are tailored for everyone who is embarking upon a job campaign. In most cases where a married person is out of work, his or her success in the job search is crucial to the mutual welfare of the couple.

In marriages where the wife pursues her own business career, it is seldom that her husband is not pursuing his own. Despite the changing role of women, men do not easily abandon their concept of themselves as the prime support of the family, and their pride immeasurably suffers when that role is threatened or interrupted. It is a real blow.

It is a real blow, too, when a career woman loses her job. She has had to work as hard or harder than her male counterpart for her achievements and the loss of a job may cause her to give in to serious self-doubt, "The world doesn't value my talents." At such a time it is especially important for her husband to be encouraging and help her keep her spirits up. She may also feel defensive if she senses that family and friends do not take her job loss seriously — because she is still a wife. Her career is as important to her sense of identity as a man's is to him.

It is a blow to the homemaker wife, too, when her husband loses his job. Her husband has been beaten by the outside world, she thinks, rejected by his firm, laid off, eliminated. What happened? Did his employers make a terrible mistake in judgement? Or was her husband himself to blame? If she is unable to cope with her feelings rationally, she may be inclined to be harsh with her husband. Part of the reason for her attack is that she wonders if it is partly her fault that he is out of a job. She feels helpless.

Whenever a man or woman loses a job, there is a tendency for the spouse to suffer from self-doubt. "Was I supportive enough? Did I make too many demands? Did I take more than I gave?" You feel helpless and think there is nothing you can do to change matters — it is all out of your control.

You are wrong. There is a great deal you can do, and your actions and attitudes are in their way as important as your spouse's at this time in your lives.

The first thing to do is understand that losing a job is a commonplace event.

The second thing to do is look upon the period of unemployment as an interim thing only and, if properly approached, a time of opportunity. When you are unemployed, there is time to define your goals and needs. No one knows you better than the man or woman you live with. It is in this defining process that he or she can be a potent assistant.

The third thing to do is realize that the way to find a new job lies in an attitude of self-confidence, the confidence to take the necessary steps which will lead to employment. Making contacts and seeing people, constructing a résumé, having interviews, all of this is, at best, very hard work. Someone who feels guilt and is unsure of support at home will not project the constructive, positive figure that people welcome into their firms. People are not hired out of pity. You will not be hired because you look miserable, starved, or as though your spouse wants you to be employed. You will be hired because a prospective employer sees the sparkle in your eyes, the keenness of your approach, and expects to hear a more rapid clicking of coins into the cash register if you are hired. That is simply a practical reality.

A spouse can help in tangible ways too — in all the matters of preparations discussed in Chapter 3 and elsewhere: joining in the effort to get in good physical condition by diet and exercise, helping with newspaper ads, suggesting names for the A, B, and C lists. It is also important to treat your spouse with real courtesy so that he or she will be encouraged to respond in kind, thereby limbering up that most important reflex. And above all, listen, share, be a big booster and ally and friend.

You who are reading this page right now may not be among the unemployed; you may be interested only in improving your career, moving voluntarily from one secure job into another, elsewhere or within your own firm. But perhaps you are thinking, as you read this, "Boy, oh boy, I hope *I'm* never in that spot!" My husband (or wife) would have to change so radically to be a help to me that I'd think I was married to a different person!" If that is the case, maybe your communications and your point of view need shoring up. Consider this parable:

We had as a client a young man who had many problems with his wife. This youngster had a very fine job with an important company, and he was excited about his work and his progress. So, every evening, he would run home and tell his wife all the terrific things which had happened to him that day or the things which he had made happen. He was amazed to find that his triumphs lit no fire in his wife's eyes. She did not bubble over with joy as he expected.

There was a simple reason for the wife's less than joyful reaction to her husband's victories. The girl was not illiterate; she had a PhD degree. But she had given up her career to raise babies and keep a nice house. When her husband came in brimming with news of the wonderful world he lived in, it was almost an insult to her and the occupations which filled her day. By bragging about his accomplishments, he seemed to attach no importance to hers. Here is a guideline for men: If you want to stop your wife's nagging—short of gagging her—pay some attention to her and her world. The only reason she nags is because she is not getting enough attention. If you minimize your wife's undertakings, she will minimize yours. Hard as it is for a man to grasp, she is not just sitting at home doing nothing while he is facing the world. She is fulfilling her own obligations, occupations every bit as important as those of the man in the office.

A client's wife once complained to me, "You know, we really have a miserable life. Every evening when my husband comes home, the children have to stop laughing and playing and appear miserable and upset because Daddy is home. He always has had a terrible day at the office, and everyone has to feel sorry for him." That is a strange contradiction imposed on many men by their emotions. Because, if you were to ask this man why he held a job and worked so hard all day, his reply would be, "For my family. For my wife and children. So they will be happy and well taken care of, of course." Yet when he arrives at his house he casts a cloud of gloom around him: the children must be glum and unhappy because Daddy has been working to make them happy and secure. His communications—reduced to the habit of a daily groan—are a total failure.

I suggest that when you get home at night you should immediately tell your husband or wife the two most wonderful things that happened during the day. "I had a great day—the boss didn't hit me." "It was a marvelous day. We lost only ten thousand on the XYZ deal—about half the loss we expected." Talk about something constructive. Not every day is horrible.

None of us will perform perfectly, no matter how well we think and plan and act. Both roles, female and male, will be full of errors. You will stumble. But, as someone has said, "Walking is only a forward stumble." As long as you stumble in the proper direction you will reach your goal. It is human to despair, but it is the better part of humanity to fight back and show courage and confidence. And a person who has the understanding help of a partner is stronger than the one who stands alone.

This leads me to reveal a secret. Let us suppose neither you nor your spouse believe in the actions that are prescribed by this book. You do not believe, but you want to. How can you believe when you do not? Simply by applying a rule of human nature. I have said it before: Everyone believes himself to be an angel and never appears to himself as a clown. Therefore, take the action advocated by me, a man who believes. Force yourself to go out on interviews you believe will be worthless. Your spouse, though skeptical, cheers you on. And, once you have gone out on interviews, you will have to rationalize — since you are not a fool — that it was a sensible thing to do. Once you believe you have done a sensible thing, you have obtained belief through disbelief. And the disbelieving spouse can achieve the same belief and thus be of aid and comfort.

I have seen this process at work many times in my counseling life. Recently a client forced himself to follow the rules and procedures I have outlined. They did not ring true to him. He thought they were too simple. But having paid good money for the counsel, he doggedly went about his market campaign. The ritual worked. He was offered three good jobs, and then his company came up with what the client called "a sensational promotion and raise." He was faced with the pleasant dilemma of deciding whether to leave his company or to remain in a better position.

What happened was that when this man got the first offer, he underwent a miraculous change. He radiated self-confidence and, as he walked around the premises where he worked, everyone could see the aura of his belief in himself. They looked at him more closely than ever before. This new awareness of a strong and confident man generated the "sensational promotion."

It is very true that we all are so conditioned by our attitudes that anyone who has belief and faith in what he undertakes achieves his goal. History is full of examples of the fact—you can recite as many historical proofs as I can. The Bible says that faith will move mountains. But the Bible is talking about blind faith. What you can have in shaping your career, in going after a new position, is rational faith—faith built on reason, not in spite of reason, faith built on known experience, logic, proven cause and effect. You know that if you take the proper steps you cannot fail to achieve the right result.

The emphasis in this book has been on your approach to the un-published sector of the job market, where 80 percent of all jobs are to be found. That is the best place to find the job which fits you, but the avenues to known jobs—employment agencies, magazine and newspaper ads, management consultants—should not be overlooked. As noted, there are also many good jobs in government at the federal, state, and local levels; one of them might fit you.

When you are actively seeking a job, your position is firmer if you are employed, but the time you can spend on your market campaign will be limited. If you are unemployed, you can work at your campaign full time. Thus the chances for a successful campaign even out—the odds for success are very high whether you are employed or not.

It might be useful to look at the reports of actual market cam-paigns made by some of our firm's clients. The first is the report of a forty-one-year-old controller with a BS degree in business ad-ministration. He had a wife and two children when he started out to find a new job. He was employed at a salary of $16,800 with a two-week bonus annually, but he felt he was in a rut. He answered forty-two advertisements and was called in for two interviews. He registered with employment agencies and went to two interviews and three follow-up interviews, one of which resulted in some interest on the part of the employer. Working from his A, B, and C lists, he was referred to twenty-seven executives. He generated interest in seven offices and received three solid offers for his services. The first was an offer for $20,000 a year. He used this offer as leverage with the two other firms that wanted him. In the end — after a campaign which lasted from June 14 to September 21 — he accepted a position with the second firm at $23,000. He was promised a review of his performance at the end of six months with a promised raised to $26,000 and a guaranteed yearly increase thereafter.

In the second and third cases, the men involved relied solely on the referred interview. The second concerns a thirty-seven-year-old engineer who had been at work ten years with an aircraft manufacturer. His salary was $22,000. He had an MBA and a BS in mechanical engineering. He wanted another job because he was not satisfied with the challenges of his position or the possibility of advancement. After initial counseling and definition, he decided to combine an internal and external campaign. Since he was steadily employed, his time for job seeking was limited. Here is his report on his campaign:

March 28: Talked with J.J., a friend who is an engineering manager at a rival aircraft plant. From this, I received two referrals — to the vice president of an electronic company and to the vice president and general manager of a packaging company.
April 8: Had an interview with the vice president of the packaging concern. This executive became interested in me as a potential employee in engineering design, a position in which I would establish a prototype shop and work as liaison with airlines for special packaging needs. I was asked to call back April 11 for further discussion. Obviously, I did not ask for referrals.
April 11: Called back and arranged for a meeting on April 19.

April 12: Conferred with a friend, a realtor, but the interview resulted in no referrals.

April 17: Conferred with a department head at my own aircraft plant as part of my internal campaign. I was referred to a division head in another area of the company.

April 19: Toured the packaging plant with the vice president. In the course of this tour, I met one of the owners of the company. Both showed interest in me.

April 21: The packaging plant made me an offer which, including stock, totaled approximately $23,000 a year. I did not accept but led the conversation to talk of my opportunities to grow with the company, which is a small firm in business just one year.

April 29: The packaging company agreed to change my proffered title to Head of Engineering and increased its stock and cash offer to approximately $26,000.

May 8: I accepted the offer from the packaging company. Three months later, my performance was reviewed and my salary was boosted to $30,000.

The third case involves a fifty-two-year-old man with thirteen years of experience at Blank Corporation. He had spent his entire career in one industry. He had the equivalent of a BA degree in liberal arts from a mid-western university. He lost his job when his company was reorganized. When we first saw him, he was apprehensive about his age and the lack of a formal degree. After initial counseling — the process described in this book — we found he possessed all the qualifications for a successful career in general management or as an operations manager.

Following a market campaign of only four weeks, he accepted one of three offers, a position as manager of West Coast operations of a systems company specializing in the on-the-job training of technicians in industries related to the client's lifelong career. This bid, although offering a smaller immediate salary than the other two, included substantial financial opportunities through override commissions and stock options. Here is the log of his campaign:

August 13: Talked to a good business friend who heads his own business consulting firm. He promised to keep an eye out for opportunities for me.

August 14: Talked to two general managers of companies I had dealt with in my old job. Received three referrals to top-notch executives and promises of more.

August 15: Saw the senior partner of an electronic manufacturing firm who gave me three referrals. Saw the president of a transfer company who gave me two referrals. The latter also volunteered many worthwhile suggestions about possible fields of endeavor I might consider.

August 18: Saw one of my former suppliers who gave two referrals and the president of a company in the building industry who expressed an interest in having me join his firm as general manager.

August 19: Saw the senior partner of an insurance brokerage and the general manager of a manufacturing firm, both of which I had had business dealings with. Each gave me one referral to top executives and promised more.

August 20: Saw the partner of a sales consulting firm to whom I had been referred. He was impressed by my résumé and promised to be on the lookout for possible employers. Saw my family dentist, who referred me to the general manager of a manufacturing firm.

August 22: Visited the West Coast divisional manager of a graphics company. Had a three-hour interview which resulted in a virtual offer in sales management, a position involving draw plus commissions which could total $28,000 within one year.

August 24: In reply to an advertisement, I was interviewed for an interesting franchise in the area of assistance to small businesses. Had a two-and-a-half-hour talk. Plan to contact them again.

August 27: I met the western sales manager for a steel firm on a referral. We had a long talk. He showed strong interest. I left with agreement that I would see him the first week of September. No referrals asked of course.

August 28: I saw the special consultant with an industrial relations bureau to whom I was referred. Received two referrals.

September 2: Had a brief introductory talk with the western manager of a systems company specializing in on-the-spot training of technicians. I elicited strong interest. I have an appointment for September 5.

September 3: Met two directors of the business services company and discussed further details about a possible franchise. To meet again September 8.

September 5: Met the western sales manager of the systems company again. We had a long talk. I answered many questions and made a good impression. I am to meet him again September 7.

September 7: Offered management of the above company's West Coast office, covering eight western states. I was very excited about this offer and its future financial possibilities. I asked time to consider the offer.

September 11: After going back to the two previous companies which offered potential jobs [the graphics firm and the company in the building industry] and eliciting positive response, I decided that, although I would receive better immediate remuneration from them, the future with the systems company had overriding advantages. My counselors concurred. I accepted the position at $15,000 a year minimum salary plus override commissions on all contracts obtained and substantial stock options. I expect a minimum of $30,000 a year.

Summary:	Total referrals received	14
	Companies interested	4
	Total interviews	22
	Job offers	3

Counselor: *This client accepted an offer before he had time to exhaust his list of referrals. His personal attitude of quiet confidence and enthusiasm quickly developed interest in his capabilities.*

Client: *Their program built up my confidence, cleared up my doubts that my age and lack of a formal degree would be serious handicaps, and confirmed my and my counselor's belief that I had marketable assets. It was good to learn that the world still wants me. As I look back, it seems almost miraculous.*

In view of the poor response women usually get in the published area of the job market, most female clients rely almost exclusively on referral interviews.

The next example involves a twenty-three-year-old social worker. She was undergoing psychoanalysis at the time she started on her program. Her primary objective was to "make a mark in the world." During the first phase of her program, it became apparent that her strongest "success factor" was her ability to deal with people in a very result-oriented way.

Her objective was defined in terms of an executive directorship of a community service organization.

The client started her market campaign with three people she knew well and felt comfortable with, even though these were not potential sources of job offers. She also had a good interview with her former employer.

Her first four interviews produced seven referrals plus an interest in forming a new organization on a partnership basis.

At this point the client felt secure enough to discontinue her psychoanalysis. All but two of her interviews produced referrals or job interests.

Here are the final stages of her campaign:

November 5: Referred to executive director of adult education organization. Had good interview. Director mentioned she had been thinking of retiring but had done nothing about it for a year.
November 6: Wrote thank-you letter detailing reasons for ability to fill the position and suggested a second interview.
November 12: Second interview. Good meeting of minds. Appointment scheduled to meet board of directors.
November 16: Met with board. Emphasis on fund raising. Showed interest in handling that part of duties. Job was offered at $12,000 per year [client's previous salary $10,700]. Negotiated increase to $15,000 after three months, based on performance.
November 18: Accepted job after talking to previous contact and agreeing to be available for consulting on his problem of training counselors, as time permitted.

Summary: Total referrals received: 42
Job Interests: 6
Total Interviews: 21
Job Offers: 3

Counselor: *Client quickly adapted to attitudes and thinking of people in this field and elicited an unusual amount of interest.*

Client: *I learned what my strengths are and how to use them more effectively. The reference and referral technique not only opens existing doors, it creates new opportunities. It is the most effective method of seeking a job I have ever encountered, and also a vital and fundamental skill in interpersonal relations. I am now able to mobilize my energies in positive, creative, and constructive ways. This experience has changed my life.*

My final example deals with a thirty-one-year-old woman with a background of commercial art and a BFA from the Rhode Island School of Design.

Her problem was that her job as one of a number of art editors in a publishing firm provided only limited chances for professional advancement in her field, and she suffered from the usual ceiling on remuneration for women in many organizations.

Since there were no "known" openings in the area except at her level, she had to rely on personal contacts.

The client had all the basic qualifications for an art directorship and had actually taken her superior's place during periods when he was absent. She knew five or six people in the publishing field, none at very high levels. Through these she made contact with seven senior executives. On one of her interviews she was told that the art director of a major publishing company was leaving. She called a former contact and obtained an introduction to the treasurer of that company.

The treasurer said he never screened people but, because of the personal nature of the referral, he was willing to talk. The interview moved almost immediately to the subject of the art directorship. Asked about her present salary, the client followed her counselor's advice and turned the conversation toward future remuneration based on ability. On a second interview she was offered the position at a salary $3,000 higher than her previous salary, and negotiated it up another $2,000, using her counselor's methods and demonstrating above-average enthusiasm and qualification for the job.

After accepting the job, the client prepared and implemented the techniques of an internal campaign and upgraded the recognition as well as the salary structure of the entire art department.

Summary: Total referrals: 7
                  Companies interested: 2
                  Total interviews: 13
                  Job offers: 2

Counselor: *Client successfully avoided getting trapped in general attitude in her field: "Tight market, no openings." She insisted on obtaining, and obtained, the same salary as a man in this field.*

Client: *I would never have been able to sell myself if I hadn't been made to realize through objective, professional evaluation that I had all the qualifications for a considerable jump in level of responsibility.*

These brief logs of market campaigns illustrate the enormous power of referrals and the strength you have when you meet top executives under the proper circumstances. A referral campaign puts you where you must be: in the offices of executives who are interested enough in you to offer advice and who have the power to hire you. I repeat: The only way to locate yourself properly is to prospect gently through the offices of relevant senior executives, quietly exposing what you are and what you have to offer until there is a matching of interests and a job for you.

A market campaign begins with you, when you list your achievements and analyze their meaning. Your list will reveal your talents, your strongest powers, and will define the kind of work you can do with the most efficiency and satisfaction. Supplement your own reasoning with the opinions of friends and relatives. Your résumé grows out of this self-examination. It is a statement of your goals and a brief statement of your capability. In every step of your analysis you must consider what you have to offer. The question is always "What can I offer to meet the needs of an employer?" It is never "How can I get a job?" No one is interested in what you want. Many people will be interested in what you can offer.

Here is a check list to consider before you begin your search for a job:

Yes No

☐ ☐ 1. Are you focused?
☐ ☐ 2. Do you really feel qualified for your objective?
☐ ☐ 3. Are you completely comfortable with your résumé?
☐ ☐ 4. Have you studied how to make contacts and follow them up?
☐ ☐ 5. Have you a list of A, B, and C contacts?
☐ ☐ 6. Have you learned how to handle an interview?
☐ ☐ 7. Have you checked your wardrobe?
☐ ☐ 8. Is your health good?
☐ ☐ 9. Are you exercising regularly?
☐ ☐ 10. Is your attitude positive?

If you can answer "Yes" to every question, you are ready to go.

Use this check list after each interview:

Yes No

☐ ☐ 1. Have you sent a thank-you letter?
☐ ☐ 2. Did you tie down your next action prior to leaving the interview?
☐ ☐ 3. Have you written letters to each referral given?
☐ ☐ 4. Did you commit any of the following errors?
    a. Talk too much?
    b. Tell your interviewer how to run his business?
    c. Become defensive over some criticism?
    d. Lack enthusiasm?
    e. Press the interviewer for a job?
    f. Talk too much?

If your answers 1 through 3 are "No," get busy.

If you answered "Yes" to any of the items in question 4, go thy way and sin no more. Thank-you letters and letters to new referrals should be written immediately after the interview.

Thus ends the book. You have very great powers. Recognize them, gather them, bring them to bear on a goal you have chosen in a common-sense way. Know thyself. Fix a goal and make a plan. If you are positive, constructive, enthusiastic, courteous, and know where you are going you will not fail. You must succeed — and you will.

Appendix—
Ten Sample Résumés

1

QUALIFIED BY:

A background that illustrates the ability to plan, organize and communicate. A competitive achiever, able to inspire confidence and productivity in fellow workers. Dependable and reliable, welcomes the opportunity to be measured by performance.

EDUCATION:

M.A. Social Science—Public Administration, UNIVERSITY OF ——— B.S. Agriculture, UNIVERSITY OF NEBRASKA, Lincoln, Nebraska   1968

EXPERIENCE:

Lieutenant, U.S. NAVY   1968 to 1976
Naval Aviator stationed aboard the USS ——— and at the ——— Naval Air Station. Employed in a wide variety of administrative training and flying duties. Assigned as an instructor in the advanced use of weapons, combat flying, aircraft systems and safety. In addition to the duties that were largely military in nature, acted as public affairs officer, assistant administration officer, education service officer and counseled junior officers. Sold and promoted a number of education and training programs.

During this service period some of the awards and recognitions received were:
• Recommended for early promotion to Lieutenant Commander
• Flew 1,500 hours as a Navy Fighter Pilot with 145 combat missions
• Received 10 air medals, 4 Navy commendation medals and the Navy Unit Commendation
• Rated first of 100 pilots in carrier landings aboard the ———

PERSONAL:

Age 30 . . . Married, 1 child . . . Excellent health . . . 5' 11" . . . 175 lbs.

COMMENTS BY OTHERS:

"An exemplary gentleman, possessed of the very finest sense of personal morality and honor. He is capable of unabated performance as a leader and manager   ——— CDR, U.S. Navy

"Exceptional ability to get along with people. Reacts calmly to emergencies and pressure situations."   ——— LCDR, U.S. Navy

"A conscientious attitude is ———'s trademark. He continually strives for perfection and self-improvement"   ——— CDR, U.S. Navy

EFFECTIVENESS

MANAGEMENT:

Developed and implemented a training program schedule that reduced replacement pilot training from approximately 52 weeks to 26 weeks while improving the quality of training.

Responsible for daily administration of ground and flight training events for 120 permanent instructors and replacement aircrews. As a result of this performance was ranked in the top 1% of officer corps.

METHODS, CONTROLS, PROCEDURES:

Conceived and managed a flight training qualification program for replacement crews that reflected its safety aspects in a record of 17,000 accident-free hours and receipt of the Chief of Naval Operations Aviation Safety Award.

Established and maintained, as assistant administrative officer, an inventory system that was rated as "an error-free system."

COMMUNICATION:

Conceived, conducted and wrote an aircraft system training manual that was used in the training of replacement pilots.

Conducted numerous training programs and lectures that received the following comments in a quarterly fitness report: "His professional manner in addressing a large class or an individual senior officer is one of extreme confidence and authority."

PUBLIC RELATIONS AND HUMAN RELATIONS:

Established and implemented a shipboard training program aboard the USS ———, for enlisted men, that resulted in 12 men receiving their high school degrees.

Effectiveness in public relations is further illustrated by:

- Acting as public affairs officer for squadron events of interest to the public, crew families, and improvement of squadron morale.

- Representing the Navy to a public school concerning Naval aviation.

- Briefing C.A.P. members on Naval aviation.

- Indoctrinating newly arrived personnel in a program that "received notable mention as one of the few human relations programs observed to be successful."

2

LEGAL COUNSEL FOR MINORITIES AND THE UNDERPRIVILEGED

QUALIFIED BY:

A deep interest in supporting the legal rights of underprivileged people, through courtroom proceedings, counseling and practical advice. Excellent communication abilities and forensic aptitudes.

EDUCATION:

J.D., —— School of Law
Dean's Award for Service to the School
Member of the Clinical Board
Secretary of the Student Bar Association
School Representative to the Law Student Division of the American
    Bar Association
School Delegate to the National Conference of Women in the Law

B.A. Political Science, University of California at Los Angeles
Dean's List
Member of the UCLA Tutorial Program

EXPERIENCE:

Clinical Affiliations, —— School of Law
Certified Law Student
Jail Legal Assistance
Intern for —— City School Attorney's Office
Intern for Equal Rights Advisors
Intern for —— Park Legal Clinic   (1974 to 1975)

Assistant Manager, Restaurant, —— Department Store,
Fashion Valley, San Diego, California
Responsible for training and supervising over 30 employees, cash flow and
public image; substitutes for Manager when necessary.   (1973 to present)

Instructor, Seventh and Eighth Grades, —— and —— School Districts,
California
Taught Mexican-American and other minorities social studies, reading and
mathematics. Responsible for program planning, initiating new curricula
and establishing and maintaining rapport, confidence and good human
relations in class of 35 students.   (1970 to 1972)

Playground Director, —— City Schools
Responsible for planning, organizing and implementing new and existing
recreational programs which included arts and crafts, drama, folk dancing,
athletic tournaments and field trips. Participants consisted of over 100
multi-racial boys and girls.   (1967 to 1972)

LEADERSHIP AND DECISION MAKING:

Selected to supervise the Law School's Clinical Board, placing sixty students in fifteen agencies per semester. As a board member co-authored the by-laws of the organization and developed an evaluation profile for each student placed resulting in continued effective placement of students throughout the program.

Supervised and implemented a varied recreational program on a daily basis in multi-racial neighborhoods. Because of the success in increasing participation in these programs was transferred to different areas of Los Angeles to initiate similar activities.

Rose to a position of responsibility in a restaurant including scheduling employees, hiring new employees and arbitrating disputes that resulted in freeing the manager to take a month's vacation for the first time in six years.

RESEARCH AND ANALYSIS:

Participated in a legal internship program preparing memoranda covering school law, contracts, property law and public relations; drafting legislation and speeches for the school's attorneys so effectively that a woman attorney was hired for the first time upon my departure from the internship.

Developed social studies curricula and worked on a report card reformation in an atmosphere using team teaching, non-grade, modular scheduling and was asked to be the team leader teacher despite my lack of seniority.

Counseled over fifty inmates in the county jail, establishing a friendly and constructive rapport with hostile and mistrusting individuals, thus receiving commendation from the supervising attorney.

RESOURCEFULNESS:

Developed, instituted and supervised the innovative "Law Student–High School Program," placing law school students for the first time in San Diego schools to introduce and explain the law to the high school students.

Organized trips to Europe and Australia on meager budgets.

PUBLIC AND INTERPERSONAL RELATIONS:

Represented the school at district-wide conferences, speaking on the school's behalf while communicating with other schools and the American Bar Association.

Organized and ran a membership drive that increased membership in the LSDABA over thirty per cent from the previous year. Coordinated a grant request that resulted in a grant from the American Bar Association to the Clinical Board.

PERSONAL:

Age 27, married, excellent health

Affiliations: ——— Bar Youth and Law Committee, Lawyer's Club of ———
Hobbies: Tennis, golf, gourmet cooking, theater, reading

ASSISTANT DIRECTOR/MANAGER
PERSONNEL—TRAINING—SOCIAL SERVICES

QUALIFIED BY:

A background of education and related experience that illustrates a high level of competency in communications, evaluation, advising and counseling, research and reporting. A result-oriented organizer, able to lead, and establish resultful interpersonal relationships. Radiates a positive and quality image.

AREAS OF COMPETENCY INCLUDE:

- Data Analysis
- Public Speaking
- Behavioral Assessment & Remediation
- Personnel Selection
- Teaching/Training
- Professional Writing

EDUCATION:

Ph.D. candidate (Developmental Psychology), UNIVERSITY OF ——

M.A. (Psychology), UNIVERSITY OF HAWAII, Manoa Campus, Honolulu, Hawaii

B.A. (Psychology) magna cum laude, UNIVERSITY OF ROCHESTER, Rochester, New York

Participant National Science Foundation Program, COLUMBIA UNIVERSITY, New York, New York

Holds California Community College Instructor and Counselor Credentials

EXPERIENCE:

In parallel with college education:

Developmental Psychology Intern
—— Diagnostic and Observation Center, Honolulu, Hawaii
Participation case studies of preschool children with learning problems

Research Assistant
—— EARLY EDUCATION PROJECT, and MENTAL HEALTH PROJECT, ——

Psychological Technician
—— HOME HOSPITAL AND TRAINING SCHOOL, ——

Instructor, Lecturer and Teaching Assistant
UNIVERSITY OF ——

PERSONAL:

Age 26 . . . Married, no children . . . Health excellent.

EFFECTIVENESS

MANAGEMENT AND METHODS:

Planned and conducted a series of bi-weekly seminars for faculty and students in the Developmental Psychology Department. This provided a new and fertile ground for creative faculty-student interaction.

Refined a means of rating the level of reading comprehension shown by children's written answers to questions about what they had read. Utilizing all of the daily reading assignments produced by a class in six months, developed a method for reducing the data in terms of the rating scale. The results, clearly presented in graph form, indicated needed direction for teaching and further research.

COMMUNICATIONS:

Delivered a paper based on my senior thesis to the Southeast Psychological Association that was subsequently published in *Psychological Reports.*

Delivered a paper based on original research to ——— Psychological Association. Was commended by the president of the Association for an outstanding presentation.

Played a key role in developing and administering a questionnaire on parents' perceptions of child behavior that enabled the Primary Mental Health Project to gain perspective on the effectiveness of the program in the Rochester schools. The questionnaire also opened channels of communication between the Project personnel and members of the community it served.

HUMAN RELATIONS:

Presented stimulating and thought-provoking lectures and demonstrations to students in a Developmental Psychology class. At the end of the quarter, a number of students stated that the class had been instrumental in their decision to major in psychology.

Hired, trained and supervised waitresses for Catering Service. The resulting increase in efficiency and organization met growth demands and prompted the Head of the Food Services to announce that I had been instrumental in achieving a new level of excellence.

RESOURCEFULNESS, PROBLEM SOLVING:

Faced with an extremely limited budget for a summer arts and crafts program, contacted local merchants for things they would normally have thrown away, and thus provided the materials for the most creative and enjoyable arts and crafts program the camp had ever had.

Demonstrated that an apparently retarded boy was not, but instead lacked sufficient stimulation. Together with the other members of the diagnostic team, I then was able to provide treatment which produced a gain of 70 points in the child's verbal IQ score.

4

QUALIFIED BY:

A background that illustrates superior talent in oral and written communications, supported by investigative thoroughness and the ability to organize multi-faceted information cohesively. Self-motivated, with public relations skills and pose. Would make contributions in all communications areas, image building and public relations.

EDUCATION:

B.A., Political Science, —— University, December, 1976.
Area of emphasis: Personnel Management.
Minors in Public Administration and Speech Communications.

HONORS:

Recipient, —— Award in Mass Communications. Scholarship finalist. Service Award, San Diego State University. Numerous awards in competitive speaking at local and state levels during five years competitive speaking. Qualified for college division Nationals. Past President, National Forensic League. High School Class Valedictorian. Life Member, California Scholarship Federation.

EXPERIENCE:

Concurrently with college education:

Supervisor, Catalogue Sales, ——. Approved checks and return vouchers, notify customers of irregularities in orders. Established a coded index system for identifying printed errors in the catalogue. The result was a 5% reduction in returns due to incorrect catalogue description. Promoted from:

Salesperson. Took customer orders, operated Friden terminals, finalized catalogue sales, accepted returns. Promoted from:

Marker. Checked incoming stock, priced and stamped merchandise, changed price tags, took inventory.

ADDITIONAL SKILLS:

Fluent in Spanish, knowledge of French, Fortran and Basic Time-Sharing computer languages.

QUOTES BY OTHERS:
>"Extremely creative, versatile, most sensitive to others and their needs."

>"Goal-oriented, strongly committed and persistent. Excellent ability with others, persuasive without seeming aggressive."

>"Consistently shows genuine interest in working with others."

PERSONAL:
>Age 20, single, no dependents, 5' 3'', 103 lbs.

5

ADMINISTRATOR
PERSONNEL, PUBLIC RELATIONS, EMPLOYER-LABOR RELATIONS

QUALIFIED BY:
>A background of specialized training and experience that illustrates the ability to develop and administer a wide variety of programs, and to select, train and motivate people. A practical, problem-solving administrator with a solid background in negotiations, labor relations and arbitration.

EXPERIENCE:
>*Field Representative,* ———, California
>Responsible for organizing classified (non-instructional) school employees in ——— and ——— Counties. Counsel employees on organizational benefits and employment rights and benefits. Represent local units in contract

negotiations, grievance matters and employment disputes. Conduct workshops and institutes, provide liaison with school boards and administrators.

1964 to Present

Major, U.S. MARINE CORPS   1936 to 1964

- *Personnel Officer*, Marine Corps Base, ———, California
Responsible for assignment and placement of 6,000 officers and enlisted personnel.

- *Administrative Officer* for the Commanding General, Marine Corps Air Station, ———
Responsible for administration of all phases of the base. Required knowledge of the functions of all departments.

- *Administrative Officer* for the Commanding General, Marine Corps Air Station, ———
Responsible for all administrative functions of the base. Represented the Commanding General at staff meetings.

EDUCATION:

B.A. (equiv.), INSTITUTE OF INDUSTRIAL RELATIONS, UNIVERSITY OF CALIFORNIA, Los Angeles

U.S. MARINE CORPS SCHOOLS in Personnel and Management, & Industrial Management

Designated *Trainer* in Labor Management, State of California

Licensed Real Estate Salesman

Course in Property Management and Appraising

COMMENTS OF OTHERS:

"Materially assisted in the growth of CSEA over the years. Cheerful . . . acquitted responsibilities well. Service and loyalty appreciated."

"Excellent ability to negotiate and to get along with people. Always diplomatic and tactful, yet managed to get his point over. A most worthy representative for his organization."

"Intelligence—diplomacy—tact—ability to get to the heart of the problem. For 14 years our relationship has been on opposite sides of the table, but always found him able to see other's point of view. An extremely capable individual."

EFFECTIVENESS

MANAGEMENT:

Assigned jobs and arranged housing, feeding, training, medical care and auxiliary services for over 6,000 personnel at the largest Marine Corps

Artillery base. As a result of superior performance, the base command received high ratings from the Inspecting General on two successive annual inspections.

Coordinated the organization, membership drives, salary and benefit presentations, insurance programs, grievance proceedings and other activities of forty-two local chapters of the ——— Association. Membership has grown so dramatically in a five-year period that eight additional field representatives are now required to handle these responsibilities.

PUBLIC RELATIONS:

Organized political action groups to support and raise funds for legislators favorable toward the ———. The association provided fund-raising personnel, telephone solicitors, volunteer office personnel and other support in the successful election campaigns of six candidates.

Represented a school employee in a dismissal action. Insured that prescribed legal steps were followed, and that the hearing was fair and properly conducted. Although the man was deservedly dismissed, he was counseled in correcting his problem so well that he was then rehired, and is currently a trusted employee of the same district.

RESOURCEFULNESS:

Utilized a variety of techniques to interest school employees in forming local chapters of ———. Potential members ranged from American Indian employees of schools near the California-Arizona line and Mexican-Americans in San Ysidro, to relatively affluent, conservative residents of La Mesa and La Jolla. Successful application of these techniques brought about the organization of some 40 units throughout Southern California.

Amassed and presented a volume of supportive evidence to convince a district superintendent to support the chapter position on fringe benefits in a salary negotiation package. After some 8 to 10 sessions the superintendent was won over, and his position was accepted by the governing board, granting the employees a substantially improved benefit package.

COMMUNICATIONS:

Persuaded a school board, that was refusing to recognize any employee organization, that the local ——— chapter was properly representative of the classified employees under legal criteria. As a result, the unit was recognized.

Conducted productive campaigns to get letters and telegrams in support of specific legislative programs to assemblymen and state senators. Aided in the passage of numerous bills of benefit to school employees.

PERSONAL:

Age 58, health excellent. Married. Affiliations: Member, Toastmasters; President, ———Club; former school board president.

QUALIFIED BY:

A background of experience in data processing that demonstrates the ability to devise and implement work improvements. Result-oriented and cost-conscious, utilizes exceptional communications skills in dealing with all levels. A self-motivated organizer who welcomes evaluation on the basis of performance.

EXPERIENCE:

Data Processing Operations Manager, ———

Responsible for all aspects of the management information system, including computer operations, data entry and control. Utilize and schedule an IBM 370/135 under DOS/VS operating under power with five program partitions, on a 24-hour, seven-day work week. Supervise up to 40 employees. Recommend and implement all hardware enhancements and placement, coordinating closely with IBM field engineers and corporation's physical planner. Order operating supplies, participate in development of department's annual operating budget. Promoted from:

Computer Programmer/Analyst

Wrote and maintained programs in PL/1 and Assembler languages. Coordinated activities with users and systems analysts. Assumed responsibility for timely completion of projects to established deadlines. Responsibilities included the sales audit system, payroll, inventory, accounts payable and receivable. Promoted from:

Computer Operator   (1970 to Present)

Prior experience as a *Water Filtration Plant Operator*, and *E-5*, U.S. Army.

EDUCATION:

B.S. (Candidate Spring 1977), Business Administration Information Systems, ———.

A.A., Data Processing (3.0 GPA), ——— College.

IBM Certificates for courses in operations management, virtual storage and operations systems.

PERSONAL:

Age 31 . . . Married . . . 5' 9" . . . 155 lbs. . . . . Health excellent.

EFFECTIVENESS

MANAGEMENT:

Monitored the cost of all data processing supplies for two years with the goal of obtaining the lowest possible prices without sacrificing quality. As Data Processing Operations Manager, phased out the company's major supplier of data processing supplies because of the vendor's inability to maintain competitive prices. Saved over $5,000 the first year by enforcing vendor competition in the area of data processing supplies.

Supervised operations staff of up to 40 persons. Hired and directed the training of ten operators and control clerks over a two-year period.

METHODS:

Headed a project which modified an inventory system to support catalog sales generated through outlying independent retailers. Produced income in previously untapped markets.

Developed job descriptions and responsibilities for all subordinate positions and brackets within area of management control.

RESOURCEFULNESS:

Convinced management to employ contract labor to process softlines sales data rather than more technical permanent personnel. Directly resulted in a less expensive, more reliable procedure with an increase in department morale.

- Bartered obsolete equipment for computer media products such as tapes, tape racks and a tape labeling system, in order to conserve budgeted funds.

- Purchased a used computer tape vault rather than a new one, resulting in a savings of over $2,000.

TECHNICAL APPLICATIONS:

- Responsible for all modifications and enhancements of the automated sales audit system over a period of two years.

- Assisted in conversion of ——— IBM 2314 disk files to an IBM 3330 MODI disk system, including program modifications, job control changes and disk file reblocking.

- Planned and supervised the conversion of all computer peripheral equipment including disks, tapes and printers.

Developed the plans for computer room expansion and optimum computer hardware placement, estimated air conditioning and electrical needs, obtained cost estimates and supervised all phases of conversion. Resulted in a smooth conversion without impacting production schedules.

7

VICE PRESIDENT, ADMINISTRATION—INSURANCE
OR
CORPORATE INSURANCE MANAGER

QUALIFIED BY:

20 years of Key Executive experience in all phases of Casualty, Property and General Insurance. Background includes broad knowledge in the areas of claims, fleet management, safety, law and contracts, insurance legislation, and training.

EDUCATION:

- J.D., Law—University of Iowa
- B.A., History—University of Iowa
- Chartered Property Casualty Underwriter—1971
- Member Iowa State Bar Association
- Member Federal Bar—U.S. Court of Appeals, 5th Circuit

EXPERIENCE:

Director of Administration, ——— INSURANCE COMPANY
Responsible for supervising 15 people in the investigation and settlement of all personal injury, property loss and damage claims for the company policyholders. Also supervise: safety program, car fleet program, and act as Oregon Insurance Legislative Director. Substitute for Executive Vice President in his absence. (1962 to present)

Claims Attorney, ———, Lincoln, Nebraska
Responsible for directing 18 employees in the investigation and settlement of all personal injury, property loss and damage claims involving policies issued by the company. (1960 to 1962)

Prior experience as *Claims Examiner* for ——— INSURANCE COMPANY; *Vice President—Underwriting* for ——— CASUALTY COMPANY, and *Underwriting Manager* for ——— INSURANCE COMPANY.

PERSONAL:

Age 55 . . . Married . . . 5' 9" . . . 170 lbs. . . . . Excellent Health.

Past President, ——— Underwriters Service Co. (Industry Association)

COMMENTS BY OTHERS:

"His ideas are sound and practical. . . . Superior ability to get along with people." ———, President, ——— Insurance Co.

"Technical ability and ability to deal with others excellent." ———, General Manager, ——— Insurance Fund

"One of the best managers I have observed. . . . He demands results. . . . excellent creative ability." ———, CLU, Vice President, ——— Life Insurance Co.

EFFECTIVENESS

MANAGEMENT:

Key member of management team that took ——— from a negative net worth to positive net worth of $2 million with assets of $8 million. Contributions from my activities were such improvements as:

- Designed the first Workmen's Compensation group for agriculture in Oregon through the State Fund which has resulted in $4 million in savings to the group and over $1 million income to the Company.

- Reviewed and approved the hiring of all key management personnel during the turnaround period.

- Established and implemented policies and procedures that increased claims handling efficiency by 60 per cent.

Developed a program as Underwriter for ——— that increased profits by $1.2 million in my first year as Underwriting Manager.

COMMUNICATIONS:

Operating as ——— Insurance Legislative Director for ——— and the industry, convinced the Legislature of the benefits of:

- Retaining the "Guest Statute" in force.

- Enacting a reasonable "Comparative Negligence Law."

- Enacting "Third Party Cross Complaint Laws."

Conceived and wrote the following manuals that are still in use at ——— which speeded up processing by 50%:

- Claims Manual

- Office Procedure and Training Manual

CREATIVITY:

Confronted with an expense problem, conceived and implemented a plan of using part time clerical help that cut office expenses by 12%.

Revised procedures that allowed ——— to reduce policy issuing time from 30 days to 5 days.

PUBLIC RELATIONS:

In behalf of the public and the insurance industry, promoted and guided legislative approvals of:

- A "Homeowner Policy" thru changing the rating laws that reduced rates and broadened coverage.

- A special category of "Workmen's Compensation Insurance" for Agriculture that resulted in a 50% rate reduction for farmers.

PROFIT CENTER MANAGEMENT/BUSINESS DEVELOPMENT

QUALIFIED BY:

A background that illustrates the ability to play a dynamic lead role in any industry and impart profitable direction and expansion. Welcomes the opportunity to be challenged by difficult situations and be measured by results.

EXPERIENCE:

President, ———, Minneapolis, Minnesota   (1971-1976)
Responsible for entire operations of this manufacturer of prestigious hydraulic and pneumatic systems and components. Encompassed marketing, plant management, credit and banking relations—extensive international travel establishing marketing/licensing agreements with major international companies.

Executive Vice-President/Treasurer   (1969-1971)
———, Minneapolis, Minnesota
Managed marketing, advertising and sales promotion activities for this steel fabricator and supplier of building materials. Responsible for all operations of the company's 200,000 sq. ft. facility and 450 employees with annual volume $10,000,000.

Executive Vice-President   (1966-1969)
———, Minneapolis, Minnesota
Third largest manufacturer of beverage and vending dispensing equipment, employing directly over 2,000 employees, with plants in the United States, Italy, England, West Germany and Spain. Developed world-wide corporate marketing objectives for sales personnel and responsible for new product planning, introduction and production. Selected regional distributors. Coordinated corporate human relations programs, and various community public relations activities. Annual volume $40,000,000.

Previous Experience—Includes *Divisional Manager,* ———, INC., Minneapolis, Minnesota; *Plant Manager,* ——— CORPORATION, New York, New York; *Associate Editor,* ——— MAGAZINE, New York, New York.

EDUCATION:

University of Minnesota—Economics/Business Law major
Member of University of Minnesota Alumni Association
Numerous graduate business courses
American Management Association Seminars
IBM Computer School for Corporate Presidents

PERSONAL:

Age 52 . . . Married . . . Excellent Health.

AFFILIATIONS:
- Sertoma International
- Administration Management Association
- Associated Industries
- Citizens League of Minneapolis
- Society for Industrial Security
- Citizens Committee—United Nations
- Minneapolis Chamber of Commerce
- Armed Forces Communications Committee

EFFECTIVENESS

MANAGEMENT:

Invited by a group of investors headed by one of the founders of the ——— Company to take over ——— Inc. that was in a state of insolvency. Completely reconstructed company's marketing approach to the industry. Devised an international system of distribution resulting in a sales increase of 40% over each preceding year for 4 consecutive years. Increased company's gross profit from 22% to 45% in the first three years. Developed budget controls and long-range financial requirements for company investors.

At ——— Company initiated marketing-manufacturing credit and inventory controls to achieve a corporate profit of over $1,000,000 with increased market equity evaluation that drove stock from $18 per share to over $100 per share.

At ——— reorganized this old family operation so that for the first time in 40 years controlled production cost per contract and established delivery schedules to form a basis for what is now a profitable and up-to-date operation.

MARKETING AND PRODUCT DEVELOPMENT:

Examples of business development are:

- Developed marketing plans for new products introduced by the ——— Company. Involved planning strategy, advertising, promotion and sales campaigns. Efforts increased sales from $18,000,000 to $40,000,000 over a two-year period.

- Established world-wide marketing agreements in the Far East and Europe for ———, Inc., and the ——— Company which provided millions of dollars of profitable volume.

- Made ——— sole source for special items to outstanding list of companies to include ———, major medical diagnostic equipment manufacturers and worked with ——— on numerous projects.

RESOURCEFULNESS:

Have successfully undertaken and personally led negotiations with unions such as ——— and ——— workers to effect a record of virtually "no strikes," "walkouts" or major grievances and have received personal commendations from unions.

Through personal intervention at top administrative level, achieved forgiveness for $100,000 plus punitive tax lien against an out-of-state corporation.

PUBLIC RELATIONS:

Have consistently played a key role in effective public relations. Some examples:

- Obtained sponsorship of ——— for the Minneapolis ——— State junior track program.

- Was elected City Councilman in ———.

- Named "Boss of the Year" by the ——— Jaycee's for community activities.

- Listed in *Who's Who in the Mid-West.*

9

MANAGER, PROMOTION AND/OR MERCHANDISING

QUALIFIED BY:

A background that illustrates the ability to plan, organize and implement, to motivate others, and to gain cooperation and respect. Highly motivated and resourceful, with the initiative and drive to establish and maintain a high level of results.

EXPERIENCE:

Operating Assistant Buyer, ———, Los Angeles   (1973 to Present)
- Responsibility for customer service and inventory control for all stores in the chain. Also directly responsible for merchandise selection, purchase,

distribution, sales and advertising for two home clearance centers.
Served in this capacity both in the furniture and the bedding departments.
Promoted from:

Management Trainee/Acting Service Manager
• Involved in all aspects of department store operations. Responsible for
solution of numerous operational and customer relations problems, setup and coordination of store-wide month-end sales.

Concurrently with college education:

Salesperson, ———, San Diego   (1972 to 1973)
• Sold men's wear, operated cash register, arranged merchandise displays,
took inventory.

Summer Program Director, ———, B.S.A., Santa Catalina
• Responsible for creating, organizing and implementing the activity program
for nearly 2,500 Scouts. Supervised 30 staff members.   (1970)

Supervised and conducted waterfront instructional and recreational
activities.   (1968)

EDUCATION:
B.S., Business Management, ——— UNIVERSITY, San Diego, 1973
• Dean's List
• Member, Personnel Management Association

PERSONAL:
Age 26, married, health excellent

COMMENTS OF OTHERS:
"Highly personable . . . considerable ability in motivating."
                                  ———, General Manager, ———

"A good problem solver. His intelligence, appearance and *relationship*
with people have made him a definite asset."
                                  ———, Buyer, ———

"Totally dependable. Extremely creative and helpful in areas where
initiative was needed."   ———, D.V.M.

EFFECTIVENESS

MANAGEMENT:

Supervised a group of laborers in the setup of the mattress department for a warehouse sale. The project was completed and ready for inspection days ahead of most other participating departments.

Played a key role in planning a departmental budget, matching projected sales with cost factors to maintain profitability. Provided a format for comparing achievement with projected expectations, and facilitated adjustments to minimize adverse effects of variations in the economy.

MERCHANDISING:

Utilized a multi-media approach in the campaign for a clearance center promotion, and coordinated corresponding movement of sale merchandise so that a gain of more than 20% over previous sales was realized.

Implemented a plan to reduce sizeable overstocks of unsaleable box-springs by having them recovered, paired with mattresses made to corresponding specifications, and sold as sets at warehouse sales and clearance centers. Increased flow of goods and dollars for these items by 40%.

HUMAN RELATIONS:

Organized and supervised a Red Cross Blood Bank campaign in which 80% of store employees participated.

Supervised a staff of 30 members from diverse backgrounds and varying experiences during an 11 week summer Scout camp. Evaluations by leaders who had attended previous camps indicated the program was successful, inspirational and educational.

Organized sales training meetings between sales personnel and vendors which resulted in increased sales potential and reduced selling costs.

CREATIVITY AND RESOURCEFULNESS:

Aided in the selection of upholstery fabrics, and chose structural design for furniture to generate excitement, attract attention, and explore new concepts in design and appearance. Provided a mix with traditional and contemporary styles, increased customers' options, and upgraded the department's offerings.

Promoted from the ——— management training program in three months, half the usual training time.

10

QUALIFIED BY:

Where the ability to meet all levels of people, understand consumer needs with an innate sense of promotional display and good business judgement would make contributions to volume-profits and company reputation.

EXPERIENCE:

Activities Coordinator
Women in Community Service
————— Day Center
————— Extraordinaire, Past President, Recording Secretary

Assisted low income and minority men and women further their education with grants. Raised funds by acting in plays, participating in fashion shows and putting on variety shows.

Organized programs and taught Arts and Crafts to Senior Citizens.
(1972 to present)

Customer Relations Officer
Loan Department, ———— Co., San Diego, California

Responsible for handling new loans, reviewing the folders of insured and checking policies and payments. Handled client problems and complaints.
(1971 to 1972)

Insurance Underwriter
Personal Accounts Department, ———— Co., San Diego, California

Duties included underwriting on homeowners, automobile, boat, jewelry and other personal items.
(1969 to 1971)

EDUCATION:

City College, San Diego, California; emphasis on Sales Management and Interior Design
————— Business School
————— Modeling School

PERSONAL:

Age 27, married, excellent health, 5' 5", 105 lbs.

DEMONSTRATED ABILITIES

MERCHANDISE/SELL:

Played a key role in Women In Community Service by managing the marketing of goods and outreach service. Represented the organization by traveling to the educational and rehabilitation center to distribute literature and explaining its importance to their programs.

As President of ———— Extraordinaire, was responsible for representing the group with public appearances throughout the community by presenting academic awards to students, by greeting guest at dinners and other affairs, by conducting business and social meetings. Also was responsible for the administration of the paperwork and budget.

TRAIN/MOTIVATE:

Planned and developed special procedures to teach crafts at ———— Day Center to Senior Citizens who were semi-handicapped. Praised both by recipients and director for the creative results.

Prepared with Director of ———— Job Corps literature to be distributed to schools, supermarkets, non-profit organizations and foundations to recruit applicants.

PUBLIC RELATIONS:

Spoke to Rotary Club about ———— Extraordinaire concerning its purposes, plans and its projects in the community.

Gave speeches at Toastmaster meetings, impromptu and prepared, concerning the affairs of the community, state or government. Received an award of 2nd place and Most Improved Speaker.

RESOURCEFULNESS:

Developed a business plan in order to become self-employed in retail, but decided talents are better suited for a larger organization.

Helped implement the Annual Thanksgiving Dansante, given by the ———— Extraordinaire in which over 600 people attend, to raise money for Educational Opportunity Grants for low income minority students by selling tickets and ads by flyers and "word of mouth."

TWO OTHER BOOKS
BY ELI DJEDDAH:

NOW THAT I KNOW WHICH SIDE IS UP
by Eli Djeddah and Jennifer Cross
6 x 9" 138 pages $3.95 paper
"Most of us, if we are honest about it, would like to be able to persuade other people to do what we want. Deep inside us there is still the little child who clamors for attention the easy way, who would like to push buttons that could evoke predictably favorable responses. This can be done, because the 'buttons' are nothing less than eternal principles of human behavior."

    In *Now That I Know Which Side Is Up*, Djeddah offers a practical philosophy based on these specific principles by which people behave. They are time-less, universal truths which he has put together in a new way—a way which makes them very power-ful tools for improvement of self and situation.

Available from Ten Speed Press, 900 Modoc, Berkeley, California 94707
Please include 50¢ additional for each book for shipping/handling.

PAPYRUS FLOWERS
by Eli Djeddah
5 x 8" 104 pages $3.95 paper illustrated
Eli Djeddah, a nationally known expert in career development, writes poetry in a style which is very much his own and owes nothing to fashionable trends. His themes are varied but always come back to the very simple idea that the only permanent and important value is love. He is capable of subtle and extremely sensitive feelings expressed in a language which is at once conversational and yet clearly that of a well-read person capable of projecting his idea in richly varied and flowing rhythmic structure.

TEN SPEED PRESS
900 Modoc
Berkeley, CA 94707
Please include
50¢ additional each
book for postage
& handling

WHO'S HIRING WHO
by Richard Lathrop
6 x 9″ 265 pages $5.95 paper Cloth $8.95

Because most people don't know the right
steps to take in their job search, most job
seekers simply prolong their unemployment
in their confusion. Consequently there are
more than 600,000 jobs every month that go
unclaimed! The author shows the new job
seeker how to cope with today's job market
by utilizing job-hunting techniques which
produce satisfying results. Previously published
elsewhere, this is an all-new edition.

"The second-best job hunting guide on
the market" says Richard N. Bolles, author
of *What Color Is Your Parachute?*

"A fresh and devastatingly accurate analysis
of the so-called job market and an invaluable
guide to job-seekers... MUST reading for every
applicant from entry to executive levels—"
John C. Crystal, internationally-known
career analyst and consultant.

p 91   responding to " Tell me about yourself. "